PASSIONS: Sins, Spells, Secrets

The Unauthorized Story of the Cult-Favorite Soap Opera

J.T. CORNELL

First-hand interviews conducted by journalist Laila Muhammad. Additional research support provided by the BWE Media Networks staff.
First Edition
ISBN: [979-8-9989769-3-3]
Printed in the United States of America

To James E. Reilly—
your stories never died.
They just crossed over.

For the cast and crew who made the magic come to life.

For the ones who stayed tuned—
through heaven, hell,
and every commercial break in between.

And for anyone who ever thought
"This can't be real."
It was.

PROLOGUE — *A Resurrection from Harmony*

Breathe in. Breathe out.

First things first, let's get the legal mumbo jumbo out of the way. *Passions*, all its witches, living dolls, orangutan nurses, portals to hell, and the scandal-plagued Crane family belong to NBC/Universal Television. They made it. They own it. They are not behind this book.

What you're holding is strictly unauthorized: part commentary, part cultural autopsy, part love letter scribbled in lipstick on the bathroom mirror.

So why me? Because if you're going to dig into *Passions*, who better to guide you than me, J.T. Cornell. Yes, I know, I supposedly met my end baked into a wedding cake at Chad and Whitney's nuptials. But this is the town of Harmony, where the dead never really stay dead, and the truth has a way of clawing its way out of the oven. Consider this my resurrection, one last scoop from the ultimate tabloid man.

And oh, what a scoop.

Think you know soaps? Think again. *Passions* didn't just bend the rules, it snapped them in half, danced on the pieces, and tossed them straight into a volcano. If you think I'm exaggerating, remember the finale: Mt. Harmony erupting, lava rushing toward town. Only *Passions* could end like that.

While *All My Children* staged another Erica Kane wedding and *General Hospital* battled mob wars, *Passions* gave us Tabitha Lenox, a 300-year-old witch with a talking doll sidekick named Timmy. Grace Bennett's infamous tomato soup cake, which half the town loathed, though I must admit I rather enjoyed myself. Timmy shook up endless pitchers of his signature "Martimmys," while everyone politely ignored that a stuffed doll had a drinking problem. And the dark forces in Tabitha's basement, or as she affectionately called them, "the boys in the basement," made sure Tabitha kept the town of Harmony in mayhem.

The stories were so outrageous that fans screamed, critics rolled their eyes, and NBC quietly wondered if they had lost their minds.

Here's the secret. Behind every spell Kay Bennett botched and every coffin burial Father Lonigan witnessed (never mind, I just remembered he was blind) was a room full of real people: writers, producers, and actors trying to keep daytime television alive in a time when soap ratings were falling and viewers craved reality TV.

At the center of it all, like a mad conductor, was James E. Reilly — genius, recluse, provocateur, and the man determined to give daytime its last great gasp of insanity. Lisa de Cazotte, his executive producer, was steadfast in making sure the magic landed on our screens.

This book is about them. Not just the insane plots, but the brilliant, maddening, stunningly beautiful, dysfunctional family that made it possible. The backstage scandals. The co-stars who got matching tattooed wedding bands before breaking up. The impossible deadlines and wild risks that turned *Passions* into a cult classic long after it went off the air.

So buckle up. This is the unauthorized story NBC never meant you to read: the truth, the dirt, the "can you believe this actually happened?" of the cult-favorite soap opera that refuses to die.

And trust me, if anyone knows where the bodies are buried, literally and figuratively, it's me.

And in case you forgot, don't forget to "Breathe In, Breathe Out." Those are the iconic words of Jane French's theme song, the lullaby that ushered viewers into Harmony every weekday afternoon, casting its own little spell.

Breathe in. Breathe out.

But enough about me. Let's talk about the man who conjured me, and the madness that followed.

CHAPTER ONE — *James E. Reilly*

Soap operas were introduced in the 1930s, and Americans gathered around the radio each afternoon to follow serialized tales of heartbreak, betrayal, and redemption. You could say they were the original guilty pleasure. They were so popular that Procter & Gamble and other soap manufacturers sponsored them outright, giving the genre its enduring name.

By the late 1940s, as television reached more homes, radio soaps migrated to the screen. *These Are My Children* by Irna Phillips became the first televised soap, soon followed by *Guiding Light*, *Search for Tomorrow*, and *Love of Life*. Within a decade, daytime drama had transformed: faceless voices became living, breathing characters in America's living rooms.

As the medium transformed, so did the storytellers who would eventually shape it.

James E. Reilly was born on July 15, 1948, in Bountiful, Utah, amongst the transition. Raised in an Irish working-class family in the Bronx, New York, Jim's early years were shaped by Sunday Mass, family dinners, and the strict routines of Catholic school. He later recalled learning storytelling at his grandfather's TV-free home in Ireland, where nights ended with two-hour tales that left him hanging on every cliffhanger.

It was an early apprenticeship in suspense, and it never left him. It isn't hard to picture that little boy in Ireland hanging on every word, already learning how to leave an audience gasping—something he would perfect decades later in Harmony.

Curious, well-read, and endlessly inquisitive, Jim seemed destined for medicine. He completed a triple major in psychology, social anthropology, and biology. Entering medical school, a future in white coats and hospital corridors seemed inevitable—until fate intervened.

Jim was well-traveled, having explored much of Europe and collected stories along the way. As Marlene McPherson, a writer at *Passions* and Jim's protégé recalled, "He was friends with Tom Langan, who was a producer on *The Young and the Restless*. Tom brought Jim to a party where he met Bill Bell. He kept Bell entertained all evening with his European adventures. Bill told him, 'If you ever want a job writing daytime TV, you call me.'" This encounter showcased Jim's charisma and worldly perspective, traits that would define his audacious approach to soap operas.

At that party in Palm Springs, amid the desert air and the clinking of glasses, someone asked Jim, "You want to be a soap writer?" recalled his friend Connie Passaicqua Hayman, a soap journalist known to many readers as Marlena De Lacroix, in a tribute after his death. She would first meet Jim in 1991, on the set of *Guiding Light*, by which time he had risen to co-head writer alongside Lorraine Broderick and Stephen Demorest.

By this point, it was hardly his first stop in daytime. He had already written for nearly every major soap on the air: *Capitol, Ryan's Hope, General Hospital, The Young and the Restless,* and *The Bold and the Beautiful.* He had earned his stripes.

The following year marked his greatest leap yet. He became the sole head writer of *Days of Our Lives.* That role would make him one of the most powerful and polarizing creative forces in daytime television.

To truly understand his impact, it's important to note that the early 1990s were turbulent for daytime soaps. The O.J. Simpson trial dominated headlines and television screens, preempting regular programming and triggering a ratings collapse soaps never recovered from. Many viewers abandoned daily viewing, and historians often cite the trial as a turning point in the genre's long decline, feeding the growing appetite for reality-based television.

The trial proved audiences were hungry for heightened, sensational storytelling, and networks were desperate for someone who could deliver it.

Against this backdrop, Jim's bold and shocking storylines at *Days* captured attention. Carly Manning buried alive and Dr. Marlena Evans possessed by the devil sent ratings soaring. Living up to NBC's 1990s slogan, it was Must See TV.

Days climbed from eighth place to nearly overtaking *The Young and the Restless*, the genre's long-time leader. The only daytime drama to see an increase in viewership during that period, *Days* stayed at number two among the eleven soaps, showcasing Jim's creative vision as sole head writer.

Later in life, Jim gained a reputation as a recluse; though *Days* taped in Los Angeles, he rarely left the East Coast, preferring to write from his lavish homes in Amagansett (in the Hamptons) and Connecticut. He didn't want to know the actors as themselves, but instead think of them only as his characters, which he felt gave him more freedom.

Friction with Ken Corday, *Days'* executive producer, was constant. Corday encouraged Jim to write more traditional stories while Reilly leaned into the outrageous. Because Jim remained on the East Coast, Ken would travel twice a year to meet Jim in New York City, planning the year's biggest stories. Jim would stay at his favorite hotel, The Carlyle, where they mapped out storylines in his suite.

Corday, a Manhattan native and Episcopalian, often clashed with Reilly, the Bronx Roman Catholic. "We love to bump heads over things like religion," Corday once said in an interview with the Television Academy Foundation. "And of course he keeps telling me

I'm going to burn in hell. I laugh about it because I think I go to Mass more than he does. We are both New Yorkers at heart with strong personalities that sometimes don't see eye to eye."

For NBC, what mattered most was the ratings success Jim brought not only to *Days*, but to NBC Daytime as a whole, at a time when the network's other soaps were struggling—particularly the aging *Another World* and the glossy new arrival *Sunset Beach*.

With success, however, came controversy. Certain longtime fans disliked the liberties Jim was taking with their beloved characters on *Days*. Jim created a spinoff of *Days*, and although the network didn't go with it, NBC didn't want to lose him, recognizing his immense talent. They gave him the opportunity of a lifetime: to create a soap entirely of his own making, free of a pre-existing fan base to please, and they would produce it.

In November 1997, after accepting the deal with NBC, Jim left *Days of Our Lives* and began working on the bible for his new soap, which would become *Passions*. For the first time, Jim could let his imagination run free. No rules, no pre-existing fan expectations— only his vision.

The following year, NBC officially greenlit *Passions*, guaranteeing it a spot on its daytime lineup. Because Jim would be writing from the East Coast, he needed an executive producer to oversee production in Los Angeles—someone he could trust.

That December, in New York City, Jim met with producer Lisa Hesser, who at the time was working on *Sunset Beach*. He had heard wonderful things about her and met her several times over the years. The meeting clinched the deal, and soon she would be officially announced as executive producer of *Passions*.

By this point, *Days of Our Lives* had been renewed for five years. Still, it remained undecided which of NBC's two lowest-rated soaps, the long-running *Another World* or the upstart *Sunset Beach*, would be canceled to make room for *Passions*. While Jim had been told early in the process that all four soaps might continue, industry insiders whispered that NBC was leaning toward pulling the plug on one of them.

At *Days*, Jim influenced everything from set design to wardrobe and lighting. NBC was prepared to offer him even more creative control: the chance to shape *Passions* from the ground up. For that reason, he planned a rare extended trip to Los Angeles to meet with Susan Lee, NBC's Senior Vice President of Daytime Programming, alongside Lisa Hesser.

He explained in an interview with *Soap Opera Weekly*, "I tend to visualize my scenes. I will have a working model of it all in my head. I will close my eyes and I will see these characters coming into a restaurant, so the restaurant has to have a certain look. I will be in LA in the spring for a year. Both my dogs are coming."

When asked if his dogs had ever been to LA, Jim joked, "One has been to LA and that dog has been in therapy because of it. He was caught in the earthquake and has literally not been the same since. So we are telling him we are not going to LA. We are going to Denver. If he found out we were heading back to LA, forget it. I would find the dog's head in the oven with a suicide note in its paw. The other one is just too young and dumb to know what LA means."

If Jim was willing to leave behind Amagansett and The Carlyle for soundstages and sunshine, it could only mean one thing. This was not just another soap. This was his magnum opus.

Jim knew he was about to create a world entirely of his own. For the first time, he could do it without compromise. The man who made Marlena Evans levitate on *Days* was about to make a witch and a doll the cornerstones of daytime television.

Jim wouldn't just be writing a soap — he would be building a world entirely his own. And in that world, reality itself would bend to his will.

CHAPTER TWO — *Pre-Production*

With *Passions* officially greenlit, executive producer Lisa Hesser began assembling her team. Among them were producer Richard Schilling, her trusted right hand who had previously worked on *Loving* and WNET, and casting director Jackie Briskey, whose credits included *Growing Pains, Perfect Strangers,* and *Pacific Palisades.*

The first role cast went to veteran actor Ben Masters as the wealthy Julian Crane, described in the breakdown as cold, controlling, and ruthless. By spring 1999, as casting continued, Emmy and Golden Globe winner Juliet Mills, beloved for her starring role in *Nanny and the Professor*, signed on as Tabitha Lenox, an eccentric older woman with a demonic streak. Her presence gave the supernatural side of *Passions* its edge, bridging old-school television charm with Jim Reilly's daring new vision.

Other early cast members included Liza Huber, daughter of daytime legend Susan Lucci, as Gwen Hotchkiss, and Dalton James as Hank, a still-developing character set to debut later that season.

Behind the scenes, the writers had already received the bible for the show from Jim Reilly and were hard at work. NBC wanted 100 scripts in the can by the time production started. Marlene McPherson and Darrell Ray Thomas, Jim's protégés from *Days*, were brought over to *Passions* as associate head writers.

Marlene recalled when Jim left *Days* to write the bible for *Passions.* "He wanted it to be like Peyton Place, this beautiful, idyllic New England town that looks like everyone leads these perfect lives,

11

but behind closed doors there's scandal and just crazy stuff going on. He wanted to do it in a way that was a little bit of a spoof on soap operas as a whole, but still telling those important soap stories. He wanted it to be outlandish—you'd sit and just laugh at some of the things, and we'd say, 'Nope, that's not enough; we've got to go bigger,' you know. He wanted it to be batshit crazy. I had to finish out my contract on *Days*, and it lined up exactly when *Passions* was starting, so I went right over and stayed with Jim."

She added, "His bibles were better than any headwriter I've ever worked with in my life."

During his early run at *Days*, Jim lived in Los Angeles writing the soap, but after the tragic 1994 earthquake devastated the area, he told Marlene, "I don't want to stay," and retreated to the East Coast.

Early during pre-production for *Passions*, Jim had made that rare trip to Los Angeles that he mentioned in *Soap Opera Weekly*, meeting with NBC executives and producer Lisa Hesser as the series took shape. He returned to the East Coast shortly after. When production neared, NBC pushed him to relocate more permanently — something he flatly refused.

Marlene shares, "Originally, when they were going to start *Passions*, they were going to make him come out for the first couple of years. I was looking for places for him to live. I was out looking for homes, and he called me in my car, when we still had car phones, and said, 'Marlene, I'm not coming. They're not going to make me come. I'm going to stay.' So he didn't come."

Jim also included on his *Passions* writing team at that time Ethel and Mel Brez, whom he had worked with on *Days*. Nancy Williams and Peggy Schibi were also on scripts; Jim had worked with Nancy during his time at *Guiding Light* and Peggy at both *Guiding Light* and *Days*.

As casting advanced, NBC began promoting *Passions* internationally. At the MIPTV trade show in Cannes, NBC Enterprises VP Jerry Petry promised a "fresh, hip" soap aimed at younger viewers. Daytime VP Susan Lee teased on-location shoots in Paris and Camden, Maine, before production would eventually shift to Los Angeles, and hinted that the show's paranormal twist would hook a young audience.

Behind the excitement, however, difficult decisions loomed.

To make room for *Passions*, NBC canceled *Another World* after thirty-five years, a decision that stunned the soap community. "This was a very, very difficult decision," NBC Entertainment president Scott Sassa told the press. "But *Sunset Beach* seemed to have more momentum with younger viewers, so we went with it instead of *Another World*."

The move sparked outrage among longtime fans, some of whom vowed to boycott *Passions* in protest. The network was betting on Jim Reilly's new world of Harmony, and Lisa Hesser was determined to bring it to life.

With cast negotiations wrapped, it was finally time for *Passions* to begin taping. Hesser divided production into two units. On Wednesday, May 5, 1999, she flew to Paris with a small crew and actress McKenzie Westmore to film Sheridan Crane's first scenes. It was during this trip that Lisa met her future husband, Antoine de Cazotte, marking the beginning of a personal chapter even as Harmony's story took shape on screen.

Meanwhile, Richard Schilling oversaw the rest of the cast in Oxnard, California, where a full carnival set was under construction. It would later serve as the stage where the cast's first encounters would take place—a surreal playground for Jim Reilly's tangled web of lovers, liars, witches, and heroes.

CHAPTER THREE — *The Carnival*

The week after production began in Paris, a hotel in Oxnard, California, welcomed the team shooting the carnival scenes that would serve as a major backdrop for *Passions'* first few weeks on air. For most of May 1999, tents were raised, rides assembled, and rooms prepared for a group of strangers who would soon become the citizens of Harmony.

Flying in from the Miami heat was Galen Gering, cast as Officer Luis Lopez-Fitzgerald. At the University of Miami, he studied English and film, imagining a future as a writer or director behind the scenes. But his striking looks kept pulling him in front of the camera. By eighteen, he relocated from Los Angeles to New York, modeling for designers such as Armani and Valentino while juggling classes at NYU. In Miami, he continued both school and modeling. By chance, he worked on a student film with James Hyde — who, unknowingly, would soon join him in *Passions*.

Hyde was living in Miami, working on *Miami Sands* and recurring on *As the World Turns*, traveling back and forth to New York. When he heard about *Passions,* he auditioned for the role of Hank Bennett. After a fax arrived requesting that he test again—this time for Hank's brother, Chief of Police Sam Bennett—Hyde landed the role.

As the cast arrived in Oxnard, production scheduled a publicity photo shoot. Brook Kerr, newly cast as Whitney Russell, reflected. "I remember those first couple of weeks when we all just met on the set in Oxnard, and we got thrown into this photo shoot where they were putting together all the families… and they were telling us to take pictures with different people."

The photo shoot and carnival scenes were when the actors began piecing together family connections. Brook met Lindsay Korman, who played her on-screen best friend, Theresa Lopez-Fitzgerald — and would soon become a close real-life friend. Lindsay recalled, "It was neat because everyone was away from the city, working on this pretend carnival."

As friendships formed, so did the show's supernatural edge. Not everyone realized *Passions* would lean into the paranormal—until they met Josh Ryan Evans on set in costume as Tabitha's doll, Timmy. Though seventeen, Josh had the appearance and voice of a child due to achondroplasia, a form of dwarfism. At just three feet two inches tall, he had already earned recognition for roles on *Ally McBeal, 7th Heaven,* and as General Tom Thumb in A&E's *P.T. Barnum.*

Tracey Ross, known as the first spokesmodel winner on *Star Search*, had been cast as Dr. Eve Russell. She shared a humorous memory of meeting Josh alongside Ben Masters, who played Julian Crane. "Josh was talking to Ben, who was standing there smoking, looking at Josh in his little doll outfit. Then Ben turned to me, and I had just been introduced, and said, 'I'm going to have very strange dreams tonight.'"

She laughed retelling the story. "First I thought Josh was going to be insulted, and Josh cracks up and bowls over laughing. I thought, wow, what an interesting guy that he could just think that and say it out loud, and everyone took it in the spirit it was intended."

That was also Tracey's first experience with Ben. She recalled that even in that moment, she found him good-looking, charming, and with the best sense of humor, reminding her of a walking old-fashioned movie star. This was where the first signs of real-life chemistry sparked between them.

16

No one realized it yet, but the carnival shoot encapsulated everything *Passions* would become — heart, absurdity, and the sense that anything could happen.

Dana Sparks brought earnest warmth. Cast as Grace Bennett, she discovered the show's supernatural direction while reading her first scripts. "One thing that keyed me in early to where we were going with *Passions*… by the fourth episode, I levitate out the bedroom window while Tabitha's down there sewing her doll. I thought, this is great."

At the carnival, Dana also doubled as Grace's twin sister, Faith Standish. She admitted the twins were not her first choice: "First I read for Ivy, then they put me on hold for what felt like two months. When I didn't get it, I was heartbroken and so invested in it. I called my agent and said, see if there's another part, because I want to be on the show. Jackie Briskey got back and said, we want to read you for Grace. Grace is the opposite of Ivy, but we think she can swing it. So I went in and read, and they let me know really quickly this time that I got it."

Dana grew emotional reflecting on how the character reminded her of her own mother:
"Grace was just… I like to think she's the best of everything, and my mom was… that was Grace. A good person, that's the core of it, everything for a good reason."

During the carnival shoot, Dana also spent time with Molly Stanton, cast as Charity Standish, Grace's niece.
"What stands out from shooting the carnival scenes is how young and new our cast was. They were frightened and excited at the same time. I remember working with Molly early on, and she was practically tucked under my arm like a little bird. She said, 'I don't know what I'm doing, I'm supposed to be in college, and this just happened. I'm on a set and should be at Berkeley going to school, and I don't know what I'm doing.' She was so sweet, so dear, and so beautiful."

17

Likewise, Molly spent a lot of time with Jesse Metcalfe, cast as her on-screen love interest, Miguel Lopez-Fitzgerald. Before his *Desperate Housewives* fame, Jesse got his start here as the youngest Lopez-Fitzgerald brother.

Off set, the cast was still figuring out real-life logistics. Many had relocated to Los Angeles; production offered a $5,000 relocation fee. Metcalfe, Gering, and Hyde bonded and went house-hunting together.

Galen recalled, "We'd get lost, and we didn't have GPS or Waze; we were using a Thomas Guide, and we all needed to live in different parts of LA for various reasons. The bickering, 'What's the freaking street?' 'You don't know how to read this.' The three of us were all fighting and arguing about who's going where and why. We were idiots." He added with a laugh, "Jesse was the first one to see a place. He said something ridiculous like, 'I'm good, can you take me back now?' We're like, take you back? Take you back where? You're with us. He was pissed off and pouting."

Hyde laughed, remembering he told Metcalfe to get real comfortable in the backseat.

Galen also remembered an on-set incident from the Oxnard shoots. "I was really trying to get into my cop thing, so at one point I handcuffed Jesse to a bench. And that was the exact moment they called us. Production was already super behind. Well, I didn't have the key. It took them twenty minutes to find it, and they were not happy. Don't handcuff your little brother to a bench when you're needed in a scene. I thought I was going to get fired that day."

By the end of May, production wrapped in Oxnard. A smaller team then flew to Camden, Maine, to capture exterior shots that gave Harmony its New England identity—postcard harbors, cobblestone streets, and leafy backdrops.

In June 1999, production officially moved into Radford Studio Center in Los Angeles. Two large soundstages became the Crane mansion, the wharf, the Book Café, and other sets fans would come to know and love. The carnival had been Harmony's first breath. Camden provided its face. Now Radford would decide if *Passions* could truly live.

CHAPTER FOUR — *Fireworks*

While the cast and crew worked tirelessly at Radford Studios, on-air promotions for *Passions* began teasing that "the real fireworks start after the Fourth of July." Publicist Eva Demirjian had been hustling for weeks, rolling out a campaign that spanned glossy magazine spreads, splashy TV promos, and even a first-look segment on *Access Hollywood*. If Reilly was *Passions'* magician, Demirjian was its carnival barker — selling magic to skeptics. By the time NBC's new soap premiered on Monday, July 5, 1999, *Passions* was already one of the most talked-about debuts in daytime television.

Just a week later, the show earned its first piece of national press when *Time* magazine ran a feature on July 12. Writer Ginia Bellafante opened with a tongue-in-cheek jab at daytime dramas—describing them as stuck in Holiday Inn–lobby sets and paternity-test clichés—but she acknowledged NBC's gamble looked unusually bold. No new soap had managed to survive since *The Bold and the Beautiful* in 1987, and with ratings plummeting across the genre, replacing the 35-year-old *Another World* with James E. Reilly's eccentric brainchild seemed equal parts reckless and inspired.

Bellafante highlighted Jim's success reviving *Days of Our Lives* with supernatural flourishes, suggesting *Passions* would push those boundaries even further. Viewers would soon meet a witch with a living doll, see heroines levitate out of windows, and watch Sheridan Crane mourn her "best friend" Princess Diana at Sacré-Cœur. For all its outrageousness, *Passions* still leaned on familiar soap staples: the

21

wealthy Cranes versus the working-class Lopez-Fitzgeralds, with ambitious Theresa scheming her way into the Crane mansion.

What made *Passions* stand out was its diverse cast and inclusive storytelling. Jim insisted he wanted "everyone to identify" with Harmony, and the first episode introduced the show's African-American Russell family not through crisis, but casually playing tennis together—a quiet but significant shift for television in 1999.

As only *Passions* could, it found controversy almost immediately. Princess Elizabeth of Yugoslavia, a cousin of Prince Charles, blasted the Sheridan and Princess Diana storyline in *Soap Opera Weekly*. "It is in exceedingly bad taste, and it's totally inappropriate." Her remarks made international headlines.

When asked to respond to the criticism, Jim defended the decision. "We're taking the most emotional part of her life and showing how our character is affected by it and ripped apart by it. I would be up in arms if I thought we were demeaning her, trivializing her death, or laughing at people who were upset by it. We did the total opposite."

If anything, the uproar proved that people were watching—and talking.

Early reviews reflected the confusion *Passions* inspired in critics. *Variety* called its plots "wacky even for the soaps"—a skeptical remark that nevertheless underscored just how far Jim was willing to push daytime storytelling.

While NBC's other soap, *Sunset Beach*, sank to last place in the ratings, *Passions* held steady—eventually outlasting it when the network canceled *Beach* on September 17, 1999. NBC had just trimmed its daytime lineup to two dramas: *Days of Our Lives* and *Passions*.

While ABC and CBS continued to carry four soaps each, industry observers speculated NBC might soon exit daytime altogether. By spring 2000, however, the experiment had paid off: NBC renewed

Passions for a second season on April 11, silencing talk of an early demise.

Variety reported that although the series struggled with women 18–49—the key demographic for advertisers—it had become a hit with teen girls 12–17, a demographic that would come to define *Passions* throughout its run.

As The New York Post wrote, "Continuing a trend that started in prime time—with shows like *Dawson's Creek, Buffy the Vampire Slayer,* and *Felicity*—teens have now turned *Passions* into daytime's most talked-about show in the under-17 set."

It quickly became daytime's top-rated drama among young female viewers.

"I don't think it's ever happened where a soap has come on and grabbed hold of any age group this quickly," Jim Reilly said at the time.

Annmarie Kostura, NBC's Senior Vice President for Daytime, agreed, "The 12–17-year-old demo is important to us because they're the next generation of viewers."

CHAPTER FIVE — *Surviving Daytime*

While viewers were coming to know the characters and storylines on the new soap, the cast and crew continued shooting at Radford Studios, home to some of the most iconic shows in television history, including *Gunsmoke, The Mary Tyler Moore Show, Gilligan's Island,* and *Seinfeld*. During *Passions'* years on the lot, they shared space with *Will & Grace, Malcolm in the Middle, That '70s Show,* and *CSI: NY*. You never knew who you might see walking across the lot on any given day.

Radford might have been buzzing with sitcom and primetime energy, but *Passions* was a different beast entirely. To survive daytime meant mastering the fastest, most demanding production schedule in entertainment.

Daytime television is grueling work: actors must memorize pages of dialogue to keep up with the relentless pace of new episodes airing each weekday. Some adapted quickly, while others struggled.

James Hyde, who played Sam Bennett, recalled how one actor stood out immediately. "Lindsay (Theresa Lopez-Fitzgerald) adapted very quickly. She really owned that character. She had a lot of dialogue," he said. Her professionalism and ease in handling scenes set a standard for the rest of the cast.

Not everyone found the pace manageable. Lindsay's on-screen love interest, Travis Schuldt, who portrayed Ethan Crane, admitted the workload was overwhelming. "I would have 30 to 60 pages of dialogue that I would have to learn in a night," Travis explained.

"When we started shooting, we would stop at 2 in the morning. I'd have to be at work at like 7:30. I wasn't able to memorize that fast, so I would go catatonic sitting on the floor of my apartment just smoking cigarettes. I would try to figure out ways to wreck my car on the way to work to get out of it. This poor P.A. would come and knock on my door and be like, 'Travis... Travis,' and I'd always pretend I overslept. He'd ask, 'Man, are you okay?'"

Jason Olive, cast as Frank Lomax—a detective and potential love interest for Whitney Russell—faced a different challenge. Already an established model, he knew Galen Gering and James Hyde from Miami, but he admits he wasn't quite sure how to approach *Passions*.

"I remember talking to Eva Demirjian. She was doing PR on the show, and I just loved her," Jason said. "I told her, I think I've been doing this wrong from day one. She goes, 'Well, it's working, so just keep doing it,'" he laughed. "I always kind of had one foot in, one foot out. I wasn't really sure what was going on."

Olive's time on the show was brief, but his experience highlighted the uncertainties that came with working on a daytime soap. Soon after, Donn Swaby arrived as Chad Harris, adding a new layer of romantic tension to Whitney's storyline.

Behind the scenes, the writers were equally adaptive. Associate head writer Marlene McPherson described how characters often evolved based on the actors portraying them.

"The character of Julian Crane completely changed because of the actor that played him," Marlene said. "Originally Julian Crane was going to be very serious and businesslike, but Ben kind of played it like a buffoon, and Jim loved that. So we completely changed that character and wrote to the way the actor was doing it because Jim got such a kick out of it. And because Jim had such an incredible sense of humor, he loved going in that direction. I mean, we went nuts with that."

The first contract actor to leave the series was Mary Elizabeth Winstead, who played Jessica Bennett, the youngest Bennett sister.

Although her time on the show was brief, Winstead has spoken openly about why she chose to leave, including her belief that she was joining a daytime version of *Dawson's Creek*. She joins a group of actors who later transitioned into major film careers and have been less nostalgic about their time in daytime television.

Between intense shooting schedules and pages of dialogue, the cast quickly learned that surviving daytime meant staying on their toes. Jim Reilly was already steering the show toward unforgettable moments—storylines that would turn *Passions* into a cult phenomenon, sending waves through daytime. One such idea was already taking shape: a prom on a boat, a spectacle poised to shock viewers and set the tone for the show's second year.

CHAPTER SIX — *Prom from Hell*

Before the start of *Passions'* second year, NBC Daytime's longtime VP Susan Lee was replaced after seventeen years by executive Sheraton Kalouria, who arrived from ABC Daytime. Kalouria had built a strong track record at ABC and was now tasked with overseeing both *Days of Our Lives* and *Passions*, guiding development and strategic planning from the network level. His arrival coincided with *Passions'* best ratings yet: women 18–49 (1.5/10), women 18–34 (2.3/14), and female teens (3.9/17).

On screen, the show's second year kicked off with Kay Bennett (Taylor Anne Mountz) scheming to win Miguel Lopez-Fitzgerald (Jesse Metcalfe) by humiliating her cousin Charity (Molly Stanton) at the Harmony High prom. The prank, inspired by *Carrie*, involved a bucket of fish guts. Tabitha, never far from mischief, armed Charity with a cursed pendant in hopes of pulling her to the dark side.

Pop culture expert Ira Madison III remembered that summer vividly. "I feel like not the summer it debuted, but the next summer once things got a little crazier on *Passions*, everybody was watching it at school during the summer, so it was a thing other kids were talking about in school," he said.

Kay and her best friend, reluctant accomplice Simone Russell (Lena Cardwell), unleashed their prank. Fish guts rained down on Charity, activating the pendant. *Soap Opera Weekly* splashed *Passions* across its cover, dubbing it "the prom from hell." Fans watched in shock as the prom boat sank, Tabitha cackled with Timmy dressed in his John Travolta–inspired tuxedo from Boogie Nights, and Charity emerged as Evil Charity.

Dana Sparks remembered the scale of it all. "That was huge. That was quite a lot to take on, and on a soap! You know? It was amazing," she said.

The "prom from hell" arc wasn't just a ratings stunt—it was a turning point, showing how far the show was willing to push daytime spectacle.

Because Mary Elizabeth Winstead had exited, a new Jessica Bennett was introduced, played by seventeen-year-old Jade Harlow. She loved joining what she called the show's "Scooby-Doo crew," the younger teen set often caught up in Tabitha's mischievous schemes and magical hijinks. Jade proudly referred to herself as the Velma of the group. "I remember when we were shooting that, the entire soundstage had been turned into a tank, and we were tied to sandbags to weigh us down, while firehoses created the storm around us. Because it was a set and lights, the cloth around the tank had been soaked in fire retardant. So it was great we had these cool storylines, but we really bonded when we were pulling these fourteen-hour days and we had this weird skin rash," she laughed.

Lindsay (Theresa) remembered how that moment was huge for her character. "Storyline-wise, that was when I finally—it took me a year to tell Ethan, that I loved him," she said.

Kim Johnston Ulrich, who played Ivy Crane, recalled bringing her son Cooper on set during that storyline. "My son was 7 and he came in, and James (Sam) was swimming around in the tank because… that James, and Cooper got down to his shorts and swam around with James. It was so fun, that was an amazing memory. The film crew even let Cooper play with the cameras on set," she said. Today, Cooper Ulrich is a cinematographer.

Brook Kerr also looked back on the shoot, proud of her own strengths. "We did a lot of underwater things, and I was so proud because I'm such a great swimmer, so I was like, yes! There were these cool underwater shots and a couple of the other people were like, uh-uh, and I was like, I want to do them," she recalled.

Her excitement underscored how the younger actors embraced the challenge, even when the stunts pushed them far outside the usual comfort zone of daytime TV.

For Donn Swaby, who played Chad Harris, the arc symbolized what *Passions* meant to its audience. "For many people that I've met over the years, they will say I grew up watching or I grew up with the show, and I think they succeeded with that intention, where they wanted a show to be that generation's soap opera," he said.

His words captured what the "prom from hell" storyline ultimately represented—*Passions* locking into its identity as a cult soap for a new generation, further cemented by TV Guide deeming it Best Soap of 1999 and 2000.

CHAPTER SEVEN — *Big Jim and Little Tim*

Passions' popularity was growing fast. Fan mail poured into Radford Studios, a pre–social media era where the measure of a show's reach was envelopes and letters rather than likes and shares. The phenomenon reached new heights when the cast was invited to appear in the Macy's Thanksgiving Day Parade in New York City.

James Hyde recalled, "Our float would pass by these young cheerleaders and these kids, the response was amazing, and I think that's when we kind of thought, hey, we got something here."

Fans quickly gravitated toward Josh Ryan Evans, who played the living doll Timmy. Timmy and Tabitha, the 300-year-old witch portrayed by Juliet Mills, became a surprise daytime duo, blending mischief, humor, and heartfelt moments no one expected from a soap. Josh's popularity was such that he was cast in the Jim Carrey film *How the Grinch Stole Christmas,* working around his *Passions* schedule. In *Soap Opera Digest*, he recalled, "I got to work with Jim Carrey for a few days, and they accommodated me whenever I wasn't scheduled to work at *Passions*. He's absolutely a comedic genius."

In 2000, at the televised *Soap Opera Digest Awards,* Josh won the award for Favorite Scene Stealer, voted on by fans. The room erupted in celebration, especially among his fellow cast members. Josh remembered in an interview afterwards, "Did you see Ben Masters (Julian) crying when I won the award? That is what we're like. We're like a big family."

In his acceptance speech, Josh thanked the women who had gotten him there—his mother, his grandmother, and his "witch," a gleaming nod to Juliet Mills sitting proudly in the audience. Laughter and applause rippled through the crowd, perfectly capturing his warmth and humor.

Passions had carved out its own place in daytime. It was not everyone's cup of tea, particularly for traditional soap fans, but as Donn Swaby observed, "People really loved the show, and it became endearing to them because it was their show, and there was no other show quite like it."

As the year closed, soap journalist Connie Passaicqua Hayman witnessed a moment she would later recount in a tribute to Jim Reilly: "My favorite Jim memory happened in December 2000, at the first meeting of Jimmy and Timmy. It occurred at the NBC Experience store in New York, when Josh was in town for a personal appearance. Not only did Jim come out of his seclusion to meet Josh, but he arrived smiling and sociable. They shook hands—Big Jim and Little Tim—just like Walt Disney and Mickey Mouse in that famous photograph. Jim dived into a crowd of *Passions* fans, accepting compliments and slaps on the back. The famous recluse was not alone anymore. He was swarmed by fans who loved what he did best: create. That is the joy, laughter, and real affection with which I will always remember Jim Reilly."

She continued, "When Timmy dressed up as a miniature doctor —remember, Jim went to med school—Jim loved inventing these outlandish situations because he knew Josh could play the hell out of them all. Timmy, created by Jimmy and brought to life by Josh, evoked pure joy. At least for me, and I'm sure for a lot of you out there."

Even an infamous blooper underscored that connection. Josh struggled to pronounce "Amagansett" on-air, requiring multiple takes —a playful nod to Jim's East Coast retreat—and it became Harmony lore. Perhaps Timmy was a little bit of Jimmy in disguise: a creator's heart made visible, living and laughing through his most magical creation.

CHAPTER EIGHT — *Two Soaps in One*

"We can go from this tender moment as a father and daughter, then go to casting spells... you get the best of both worlds." —Brook Kerr (Whitney Russell)

From its earliest weeks, *Passions* announced itself as a glorious contradiction. Earnest family drama sat right next to midnight-movie camp. Harmony's secret engine ran on tonal whiplash. One moment there was a tearful confession between parent and child; the next, a hex, a haunting, or a doll shaking up another round of "Martimmys." That unpredictability did not repel audiences—it became the hook, and fans quickly embraced the rollercoaster. Flipping through the channels in 1999 and the early 2000s, you might stumble across Timmy the doll being chased by Tabitha's demonic cat Fluffy, always heard but never seen.

Another type of whiplash was all too common in daytime television: changing faces. When Rebecca Hotchkiss first appeared, she was played by none other than Maureen McCormick, best known for her iconic role as Marcia Brady on *The Brady Bunch*. She signed on for a brief ten-episode stint, but when the character proved too delicious to drop, McCormick could not extend due to other commitments.

In her place arrived Andrea Evans, already a soap opera legend from *One Life to Live* and *The Bold and the Beautiful*. Evans' wry delivery and mischievous sparkle quickly cemented Rebecca as one of

Harmony's most reliably outrageous players, a role she would own for the rest of the series.

The same season brought a major shift for her on-screen daughter, Gwen. In November, Liza Huber announced she would be leaving the show to move to New York following her engagement. Gwen did not disappear. Natalie Zea stepped into the role, bringing a softer edge to the character for the next couple years.

By February 2001, another casting change arrived. NBC released a statement explaining that Dalton James had been let go as Hank Bennett, as the show was taking the character in a different direction. The role was eventually recast with Ryan McPartlin, who brought fresh energy and a new look to the part.

Even with these recasts, *Passions* was not content to play things safe. That March, Jerry Springer appeared in a one-off episode that epitomized the show's willingness to lean into its own absurdity. In a chaotic hallucination, Eve Russell found herself on *The Larry Winger Show*, a spoof of Jerry's real-life raucous program. She was confronted by her worst secrets as angry friends and enemies stormed the stage. It was silly, self-aware, and exactly the kind of stunt that made *Passions* a cult conversation piece. Brook Kerr went on record stating it was her personal favorite episode, saying, "Pregnant Whitney on *Jerry Springer*, all day."

Through all the chaos, the show never lost sight of its emotional core: the star-crossed romances of Theresa and Ethan, and Sheridan and Luis. Theresa and Ethan remained locked in a combustible triangle with Gwen, their love tested at every turn by family, fate, and class divides. Sheridan and Luis' passion, meanwhile, faced relentless sabotage from Sheridan's own family, with her brother Julian scheming under orders from their iron-fisted father, Alistair.

For all their struggles, these couples became icons for fans. McKenzie Westmore and Galen Gering, alongside Juliet Mills as Tabitha, even landed on the cover of *TV Guide* as *Passions* kicked off its third year. With two alternate covers of the show on newsstands, the message was clear: a show once dismissed as a novelty had cemented its place in the wider culture.

Rodney Van Johnson, who played Russell patriarch T.C. Russell, recalled, "We were going against the grain of traditional soap opera completely. We were making fun of ourselves, we were making fun of current events, we were just having fun, and people were like thumbing their nose at us, but then the ratings started to come around and everyone was like this is crazy, this is kind of fun, this is release."

Passions had proven it could be both things at once—earnest and outrageous, romantic and ridiculous—two soaps in one. That duality was no accident. It was the formula that made Harmony impossible to ignore.

CHAPTER NINE — *Dreaming Bigger*

By its third year, *Passions* was strutting. Cast members kept appearing on glossy magazine covers and pages because the hour in Harmony was doing what daytime is supposed to do: hooking viewers and refusing to let go. *Entertainment Weekly* checked in regularly, praising that the show was "...comedy, drama, camp classic, soap send-up, *Passions* works." *USA Today* nodded to its velocity, saying it "has a gift for head-turning plots." *Rolling Stone* called it a "hot, guilty pleasure." The cultural bleed was unmistakable. Even Spike on *Buffy the Vampire Slayer* was canonically obsessed with *Passions,* hustling to the TV to fret over Tabitha and Timmy. When a primetime vampire's guilty watch is your soap, you have crossed out of daylight hours and into pop folklore.

NBC's confidence in the show reached a new pitch. The network offered Jim Reilly a multi-deal he couldn't refuse. First, a Saturday morning spinoff for its TNBC block—the still-popular teen lineup that had produced hits like *Saved by the Bell, Hang Time,* and *City Guys.* Jim's pitch, *Harmony High,* would follow a new group of teenagers navigating high school, with occasional visits from *Passions'* younger cast to ferry viewers between worlds. Tabitha Lenox would serve as a den mother of sorts, reined in just enough to fit TNBC's "educational" guardrails. There was even talk of a two-way door, where a character created on *Harmony High* could later migrate into *Passions* proper.

Alongside the TNBC spinoff was a primetime TV movie of the week, a one-off special that industry insiders speculated could be a

41

televised adaptation of the *New York Times* bestselling tie-in novel *Hidden Passions: Secrets from the Diaries of Tabitha Lenox*. Though Jim was paid handsomely for the network's multi-deal, neither project would ultimately be green-lit. TNBC's ratings soon began to falter, squashing the spinoff plan, with the Saturday morning block being sold to Discovery Kids, and the primetime movie never clearing its final hurdle.

Meanwhile, on screen, *Passions* was still on a roll. The show teased a more operatic supernatural palette. On New Year's Eve, the Bennett house was attacked by ravens in an homage to Alfred Hitchcock's *The Birds*, and not long after, blood seeped through the living room walls. That spring, the trap snapped shut: a portal to hell opened in Charity's bedroom closet. To spring the latch, the show enlisted daytime icon Robin Strasser as Hecuba, a gleeful and malevolent counterpoint to Tabitha. Strasser was best known for playing Dorian Lord on *One Life to Live*. After a contract dispute at OLTL, she chose to return to California to be near her mother. *Passions* executive producer Lisa Hesser called with the Hecuba role, and the timing clicked.

In recent years, Strasser has praised the show, noting that playing full fantasy as a witch with glorious costumes and wigs was joyful and that she is still passionate about *Passions*. Her Hecuba tempted Kay Bennett, now played by Deanna Wright, into selling her soul. She then set about destroying Charity Standish by ripping open the world with a portal to hell in her closet. Viewers recognized the delight in her performance. At the televised 2001 *Soap Opera Digest Awards*, Robin Strasser won Outstanding Female Scene Stealer.

On set, the story felt as tactile as it was outrageous. "I knew we were pulling from Poltergeist, because the doorway to hell was in the closet and all that stuff," Jade Harlow said. "I was excited about that particular storyline, and the gargoyles falling through the ceiling with the slime. I was like, we're doing Poltergeist, this is great." When the Bennett house finally got sucked into hell, the prop department told the cast to scavenge souvenirs from the wreckage. Harlow walked away with four-foot candleholders for her first apartment.

Donn Swaby, whose character Chad Harris was largely grounded in searching for his parents, making music, and a slow burn with Whitney, remembers the day he crossed into the supernatural lane. "All of a sudden, Chad was thrown into this situation where he's helping a bunch of other people try to keep these demons from coming out of a closet," he said, laughing. "I remember standing there like, 'Wow, okay, so I'm really doing it now.' I enjoyed it."

Daytime's conveyor belt kept moving even as the Bennett house gave way. Fan favorite Lena Cardwell, the original Simone Russell, exited in the thick of the arc. In her *Sessions with Steven* interview, Cardwell explained that her mother, who was also her manager, wanted her to broaden her horizons. A film offer arrived, contract questions followed, and the decision crystallized. "As a manager, as my mother, she wanted the best," Cardwell said. "She wanted me to leave and try to go further." Lena landed *Jeepers Creepers 2* and other projects soon after. Her last days in Harmony were spent wrestling Kay from the closet's edge while hell raged a foot away, trying to stop her from leaping in to save Miguel. Lena now goes by her birth name, Jennifer Hazel, and is a children's book author.

Change was constant in Harmony, but the show's core spirit remained.

Chrystee Pharris stepped in as the new Simone at full tilt. Recasts are never invisible in a town as small as Harmony, yet Pharris recalls how the cast welcomed her into the family with open arms.

Strasser shared the spotlight that year with Josh Ryan Evans, who also won Outstanding Male Scene Stealer at the 2001 *Soap Opera Digest* ceremony for the second year in a row. His public mantra, "Dream Big," was not just a line he used while signing autographs. It was the way he encouraged people he met to move through the world, a reflection of the life he had carved out on screen and off.

In retrospect, the chapter tells on itself. NBC wanted proof that *Passions* could live across formats. The show proved how far it could stretch inside one. A *New York Times* bestselling tie-in novel, pull quotes from *Entertainment Weekly* and *USA Today,* the "hot, guilty pleasure" tag from *Rolling Stone,* a vampire on a hit primetime series glued to the feed. And on screen, a closet to hell. Daytime was not supposed to hold all of that. Harmony did, and it was not done yet.

CHAPTER TEN — *Still High*

Passions was still at the height of its popularity in 2001, averaging 2.4 million viewers a day and holding strong as NBC's wildest daytime gamble. The stories on screen were chaotic, unpredictable, and utterly captivating. Few episodes illustrated this better than the double wedding of Theresa and Ethan, and Luis and Sheridan. The ceremony descended into total mayhem when Ivy Crane drove her car straight into the church to stop the weddings. Meanwhile, a mysterious man named David Hastings appeared in Harmony, claiming to be Grace's long-lost husband. Tabitha and Timmy, fleeing the deranged and axe-wielding Norma, found themselves aboard a boat bound for Warlock Island with Harmony's teens for a summer camping trip. And through it all, Charity's ominous premonitions warned of danger lurking around every corner.

The spectacle never let up. The Bennetts temporarily moved in with Tabitha while their home was rebuilt, because yes, it had been sucked into hell. Sheridan and Luis' romantic getaway in Bermuda ended in a literal explosion at sea. A drunken night led to Theresa accidentally marrying Julian, and a year later, she gave birth to Little Ethan, believing the baby was Julian's when in fact the father was Ethan.

Each storyline collided with the next, in a dizzying rhythm that fans found irresistible.

While *Passions* was a hit with its devoted audience, it never earned the respect of the daytime establishment. The show was routinely snubbed by the Daytime Emmys, even as it delivered some of the most imaginative work on television. Year after year, powerhouse performances from Ben Masters, Juliet Mills, Kim Johnston Ulrich, and Lindsay Korman, among others, went unrecognized. For fans, the omissions felt personal — a reminder that the industry didn't quite know what to do with a show that gleefully broke every rule.

Soap Opera Digest once described *Passions* as "frozen in motion," a jab at the show's slower-than-usual pacing, to which Kim Johnston Ulrich laughed, admitting, "I got very smart with wardrobe because you'd go in for a fitting and you'd say how long am I going to be in this dress, especially for party scenes. It would be weeks, like four and five weeks. I'd go, 'Okay, so I have to have a really comfortable dress.' She laughs. You'd see everybody wearing strapless dresses, and I'd say, 'You're going to be pulling that up for four weeks.'"

That year brought two major arrivals in Harmony. Amelia Marshall joined the cast as Liz, who would later be revealed as Eve's adoptive sister. Her casting came with a nudge from *Passions* staff writer Nancy Williams Watt, who had worked with Amelia during her years on *Guiding Light* and championed her for the role. Having just relocated from New York to Los Angeles, the offer arrived at the perfect time. Around the same period, Christopher Douglas joined the series as Brian, whose true identity was later revealed as Antonio Lopez-Fitzgerald — the long-missing brother whose return would complicate both family loyalty and Sheridan Crane's heart.

As winter approached, the supernatural elements of the show became even more prominent. Kay Bennett discovered Tabitha's spell book and, determined to win Miguel's love, cast a spell that froze Charity in a block of ice. From this magical prison emerged Zombie Charity, a mischievous and darker version of the usually kind character.

Amid the chaos and camp adventures, one of the most emotional moments of the season occurred during the holiday episodes. Timmy's lifelong wish finally came true when he became a real boy.

For Tabitha, it was magical and heartbreaking all at once. She had loved Timmy and feared the physical realities he would now face as a mortal, sickness and hurt.

Fans were moved, and the scene underscored the unique blend of whimsy and emotion that *Passions* brought to daytime television.

During these years, *Passions* regularly outperformed ABC's *Port Charles*, a feat that did not go unnoticed. *Port Charles*, the lowest-rated soap airing at the time, attempted a bold rebrand of its medical drama into a gothic, supernatural series filled with vampires, angels, and werewolves, the very territory *Passions* had already conquered. The experiment was short-lived, and *Port Charles* was canceled in 2003. Yet the attempt demonstrated just how influential *Passions* had become, echoing the kind of genre impact that *Dark Shadows* had in the 1960s.

Associate head writer Marlene McPherson recalled how far *Passions*' reach extended beyond its daytime slot. "We had such a cult following, largely because of Timmy, that they used to play *Passions* episodes on a loop at a gay bar in New York. They played it constantly — that's all that was on."

Passions thrived on chaos, romance, and magic. It challenged daytime norms, delighted its loyal fans, and left an indelible mark on the soap opera landscape. For viewers, every episode was an adventure — a whirlwind that could only happen in Harmony.

CHAPTER ELEVEN — *From Hell to Heaven*

Passions had celebrity fans tuning into the show. Professional wrestler Dolph Ziggler, *Hamilton* and *In the Heights* creator Lin-Manuel Miranda (Pulitzer, Grammy, Emmy, and Tony Award winner), and *New York Times* bestselling author Angie Thomas were among the many celebrity fans who tuned in religiously.

Angie shared with us, "In my mind I was an honorary Russell/Crane; I wanted to be both," she laughed.

Their devotion spoke to how far the show's outrageous magic had traveled—reaching pop-culture icons as it entered its most over-the-top year yet.

When the new year rang in for 2002, Julian Crane was shot at the Harmony Cannery and fell into a vat of boiling tuna. Everyone, of course, had a reason to want him dead. *Soap Opera Weekly* splashed the cast across its front cover, leaving fans wondering: Who Shot Julian Crane?

Just weeks later, Theresa—believing she had lost Ethan forever—jumped off the wharf in an attempt to end her life and found herself in Hell, face to face with Hitler, Mussolini, and the Devil himself, played by none other than Eric Martsolf. This marked Eric's first on-screen appearance on *Passions,* buried under heavy makeup as the Devil—or, as he would later joke, "I looked like Gene Simmons on crack."

Afterwards, Eric would receive another call from producers to return as a Zombie Cop, summoned to thwart Kay's plans to win Miguel.

In true *Passions* fashion, even its casting was a reincarnation of sorts. His third appearance came that summer when he took over the role of Ethan Winthrop following Travis Schuldt's departure. Eric slipped into the part seamlessly, many fans never realizing he had already appeared in those smaller roles.

On-screen, Theresa faced execution by lethal injection for Julian's supposed murder.

Lindsay Korman, who portrayed Theresa, recalled wondering how fans would react to the show switching out Ethan during such a big storyline. "It was crazy that they switched them during the prison stuff, because it was kind of a pretty serious point in my characters life, and I was like 'oh my god how is this going to work.'"

Eric shared, "I found myself on my first day with my face up against the window with Natalie Zea coming up next to me, I'm like, who are you again? She's like, I'm your wife. I'm like, oh, well, then why am I so concerned about this woman in the chair being executed? Because you secretly love her. I'm like, okay." He laughs.

It was the show's anniversary—billed on NBC as *The Incredible Summer of Passions*—and the storylines were more outrageous than ever. Jim Reilly mentioned in *TV Guide* that the whole summer is one night, something unprecedented even for soaps.

Zombie Charity frequently broke the fourth wall, taunting viewers directly: "For those of you thinking Theresa will be saved just in the nick of time—don't get your hopes up."

It was absurd, operatic, and entirely *Passions*—a show unafraid to turn death, damnation, and fantasy into a single, seamless summer spectacle.

Theresa was executed for Julian's supposed murder. In reality, Julian was alive and well, far from Harmony. He eventually bumped into Timmy, now a real boy, on a quest to save the real Charity from a block of ice by finding the demon's horn. In one of the show's most whimsical storylines yet, Timmy and Julian set off down the yellow brick road together in a *Wizard of Oz*–inspired adventure.

Ben Masters (Julian) once reflected fondly on his young co-star. "In life, you come across people who are extra special at different times and you realize that you are in the presence of someone who is extra special. I believe that Josh is one of those people. I believe that the courage that he possessed and the courage that he used in life is something that we should all hope that we have a fraction of in our own lives."

When Julian finally returned to Harmony, the chaos reached its peak. Furious his sister had been executed by lethal injection for Julian's murder, Luis attacked him. Julian accidentally knocked over a candle, setting Theresa's coffin ablaze as horrified mourners watched —the burning body revealed as a wax figure. The real Theresa was alive, part of a twisted scheme concocted by none other than Alistair Crane.

In the graveyard, under a pouring summer rain, Zombie Charity entranced Miguel, trying to kill him through seduction while Kay struggled to stop her. The dead rose from the ground, pinning Miguel and keeping Kay from reaching him.

Behind the scenes, the crew went all out to bring the sequence to life. Special effects makeup artist Michael Burnett created six zombies, and even his wife played one of them. Burnett himself provided the zombie hands that held Jesse Metcalfe's character down. After the director called cut, Burnett gave a CD to the audio booth, and they cued Michael Jackson's *Thriller*. The crew broke into the iconic dance on set, a fun moment after a long day of taping.

On screen, when Timmy arrived back to Harmony with the demon's horn, he battled Zombie Charity in a final showdown to save the real Charity. In an epic moment for the series, the battle between good and evil was on, however Timmy and the real Charity, now fully thawed, were gravely injured and rushed to the hospital. Timmy, now fully a real boy, succumbed to his wounds in an emotional farewell with Tabitha. In one of the most poignant scenes in *Passions* history, Timmy's heart literally went to Charity—saving her life.

Because *Passions* filmed about three weeks ahead of its air dates, the episode depicting Timmy's death aired on August 5, 2002—the very same day actor Josh Ryan Evans passed away during surgery to correct a congenital heart condition. The chilling coincidence made national headlines, shocking fans and devastating the *Passions* cast and crew at the Radford Studio lot.

CHAPTER TWELVE — *Life After Timmy*

On set, the grief over Josh Ryan Evans' passing was palpable in every scene.

The show had already taped a month in advance and introduced Cracked Connie, played by Kacie Borrowman, a demon doll created by Zombie Charity. She was intended to appear alongside Timmy, though his death precluded it.

The original plan called for Tabitha to resurrect Timmy later that year, bringing him back to life as a doll. Associate headwriter Marlene McPherson explained the intended dynamic. "Cracked Connie was going to get him [Timmy] into a lot of trouble. She was going to be the bad influence. Tabitha was going to have to save him from Cracked Connie."

Director Phideaux Xavier commented, "Some fans thought we were trying to replace Timmy, which was not true."

"We were scrambling rewriting," Marlene remembered. The story was rewritten, and additional scenes of him in heaven that had been shot were cut from airing. Cracked Connie would stick around for a while, but would eventually be written off with Cecil, another companion doll played by Arturo Gil.

On screen, mourning Timmy's loss became part of the story. Julian came to pay his respects to Tabitha, and the show wove the grief into its ongoing narrative, culminating in one too many

Martimmys and a night of wild passion between Tabitha and Julian. This plot point would later explain Tabitha's unexpected pregnancy.

Chea Courtney, daughter of baseball legend Pete Rose, had originated the role of the Little Angel Girl from the first episode. She filmed her final scenes that year. Her character had played a crucial role in Timmy's journey, turning him into a real boy. Diandra Newlin would continue the role from October 13 to December 9, 2003.

Tabitha remained at the center of the show's whimsical and magical storylines. She encountered several dancing babies, each hinting at upcoming pregnancies on the show.

While she knew the parentage of most, one baby left her stumped, asking repeatedly, "Whose your mommy?" Eventually, Tabitha would discover that the child in question was her own, adding another layer to her enduring role as Harmony's mystical matriarch.

Bruce Michael Hall, who played Reese Durkee, Harmony High's resident nerd obsessed with exposing Tabitha as a witch, shared his own memories of Josh. For three years, Bruce's character was convinced that Tabitha's doll was alive, making him a key player in many of the show's funniest moments.

"Josh was such a sweet guy, and I'm going to miss him," Bruce said shortly after his death. "I spent three years chasing him around Harmony! Those scenes were so much fun—they were my favorites. A funny story was when Kay crawled into my sleeping bag and I had the kissing scene with Josh. It was during the Warlock Island story. For days before we did it, I kept teasing Josh that I was going to plant one on him! He was like, 'No!' When we did it, he turned around in the sleeping bag and I had an arm around him. He was trying to wiggle out. They called cut and I pretended I was asleep. He was just a really nice guy…the best. I'm going to miss him."

Deanna Wright, who played Kay, also reflected on his memory shortly after his passing. "The first time I met Josh, I'd only been on the show for about a week or two, and I was forever getting lost on the sound stages. It gets confusing because they always move things around and change the sets. After opening my fourth wrong door, I asked no one in particular, 'How the heck do you get out of here?' Josh came walking up and said, 'I'll make you a deal—if you open all the doors, then I'll lead you out.' From that first meeting, I knew Josh had a very special spirit, and over the next two years working with him, I learned more and more about him that confirmed my first impression."

Juliet Mills, who played Tabitha, reflected on her grief with heartfelt candor. "There's so much to say; it's hard to know where to begin. It is a very hard time for me, having to go back to work and knowing he isn't coming back to work. He's still very much there in my mind and my heart. Josh and I both realized we were very fortunate to work together. We had such rapport and were so fond of each other. It wasn't difficult to do the scenes we did and have the fun we had, and let everyone who watched share in it."

Josh's passing marked the end of an era for *Passions*. For all its outrageous storylines and supernatural twists, the loss of the show's smallest star reminded everyone, cast, crew, and audience alike, that beneath the camp and chaos, there was heart.

CHAPTER THIRTEEN— *Chaos in Harmony*

By 2003, *Passions* was still weaving its way into mainstream pop culture. Even the popular WB series *Charmed* referenced it that year, when Piper watched an episode of the soap in "The Day the Magic Died."

In daytime, the show must go on—especially in a genre producing new episodes every weekday. That year, Liza Huber returned as Gwen following Natalie Zea's exit. Zea would go on to star in *Dirty Sexy Money, The Following,* and *La Brea,* proving that *Passions* still served as a launchpad for talent.

The show also introduced newcomer Justin Hartley as Nicholas Foxworth Crane, known as "Fox," giving him his start before he became known for *This Is Us* and *Tracker.* Once again, *Passions* proved it could spot and shape stars.

By the summer, the series launched "Hot L.A. Passions," a sun-soaked arc that moved several of its central characters to Los Angeles. Gwen, pregnant, traveled with Ethan for special prenatal care from Dr. Abel—unaware that Theresa was also there with Fox, Whitney, and Chad (now played by Charles Divins). Drama erupted when Gwen caught Ethan and Theresa making out.

Meanwhile, Whitney discovered Chad had once been married to a woman named Latoya, whose cousin Puff Dog soon put all their lives in danger. During this chaos, Fox battled his feelings for Whitney. Fans embraced the unexpected chemistry between Fox and

Whitney, a pairing that quickly became one of the summer's most talked-about storylines.

New York Times bestselling author Angie Thomas recalled, "Fox and Whitney. Oh my God. The way Fox would talk about Whitney and his love for her, it was like, what? They had such amazing chemistry. And then there's this whole thing of them being so opposite because Whitney was the good girl, and Fox was the bad boy from the rich family. And then the added drama of she hates his father because she thinks her mother is having an affair with his father. I'm like, that's classic soap. So yeah, my heart aches for what could have been for those characters."

Off-screen, Justin Hartley and Lindsay Korman, who played Fox and Theresa, would soon begin a real-life romance.

As the Los Angeles stories burned hot, the supernatural core of Harmony was about to erupt again. Tabitha gave birth to her daughter Endora, a scene of demonic proportions. Kay delivered her and Miguel's baby, Maria, while Gwen grieved the loss of her own child following her confrontation with Theresa.

And then there was Beth. Once the sweet owner of the Book Café with a longtime crush on Luis, her true colors finally emerged. Though she had been a part of Harmony since the show's first year, it wasn't until now that viewers saw her scheming and manipulative side. Determined to be with him, she hatched a plan to steal Sheridan's baby and pass it off as her own, even faking a pregnancy. Her mother, Mrs. Wallace, refused to go along but was threatened with being sent to a rat-infested nursing home if she spoke up.

Kathleen Noone, who played Mrs. Wallace, recalled how the offer came to her. "The producer, Lisa Hesser, called me and asked me to play the role. It sounded so outlandish and fun, and I thought, of course I want to play something like that. Once I got into the role and saw what it was, we just took off with it. And I got to tell you, it became absolutely delicious. Delicious to play, delicious to be a part of the group. The whole cast was fun. We'd go with it. I mean, where else could I be in scenes where, in order to hide, I put a lampshade on my head and stood in a corner thinking no one would see me? Also the fact that I was an old hag, you know, with a walker and the orangutan as my nurse caregiver. So right away it set it up for me, you can be a little out there, Kath. And I loved that."

She added, "The fact that Lisa, whom I had known from *Sunset Beach*, even thought of me to do this, I was so grateful."

On screen, to make things even wilder, Beth enlisted Precious, an orangutan, as Mrs. Wallace's caretaker.

Galen Gering remembered Bam Bam, the orangutan who played Precious. "It had its own dressing room. I knew the trainers, I knew its smells and behaviors. It knew me—the whole thing."

Things didn't always go smoothly. Galen shared one memorable moment when Precious was supposed to fetch him a beer from a fully stocked fridge. "Instead, it grabbed the ketchup and mustard and started squeezing, spraying the entire set. I thought, oh my God, this is amazing." He added, "They can only work to a certain age. They're like teenagers, trying to figure out where they fit in." Bam Bam is now retired in Florida at the Center for Great Apes. But not everyone was amused by Precious's antics.

As you can imagine, PETA was not happy about Precious—nor was the Center for Nursing Advocacy, which blasted the storyline as a "degrading vision of nursing." The group argued that portraying a monkey as a nurse trivialized the profession and contributed to the real-world nursing shortage. Reilly, never one to back down, mocked the outrage. He told *TV Guide* that if nurses knew how much the orangutan was paid, they'd "all be putting on monkey suits." The advocacy group responded by giving him their tongue-in-cheek "Let Them Eat Banana Cake" award.

On screen, Sheridan was kidnapped by Beth and her accomplice Charlie, played by actress Jordan Baker. To avoid being noticed, the two wore clown outfits, traumatizing Sheridan in a bizarre charade that would ultimately have Sheridan trapped in a pit inside the basement of Beth's home until she gave birth.

When Luis, Hank, Antonio, and others from Harmony P.D. searched every home for the missing Sheridan Crane, Mrs. Wallace panicked, imagining she, Beth, Charlie, and Precious would all end up in jail. In classic *Passions* fashion, she imagined it as a musical homage to *Chicago,* in an original number called "I Ain't Sorry," which received rave reviews and even won the show a Daytime Emmy for Outstanding Original Song.

Kathleen recalled, "We had long rehearsals for that, which I felt I was back doing a show in New York. It was great fun doing that. I felt it was groundbreaking because we were bringing that to daytime."

And at the center of it all was Beth, played by Kelli McCarty, who had already lived several lives herself and had first captured public attention as Miss USA 1991. She later surprised fans again with a short-lived foray into adult film—another twist that, in its own way, echoed the boundary-pushing spirit of *Passions* itself.

Fans reveled in Harmony's chaos. *Passions* didn't just lean into chaos—it danced with it. And in Harmony, chaos always won.

CHAPTER FOURTEEN— *Double Duty*

By this time, Jim Reilly had fully entrenched himself at *Passions*, while *Days of Our Lives* slipped from its once-comfortable second-place position in daytime ratings, eventually falling to fourth among the remaining soaps. Rumors of Jim's possible return to *Days* to revive its fortunes began swirling after the July 8, 2000 issue of *TV Guide* reported that NBC was "toying with the idea of bringing *Passions* creator and head writer Jim Reilly to take over the writing of *Days of Our Lives* as well." Although the report had first surfaced in 2000, the whispers continued for years.

Ken Corday, the longtime executive producer of *Days,* was furious, immediately blasting the report as having 'no truth whatsoever.' In classic Corday fashion, he went even further, calling the magazine's reporting "malicious."

Insiders recalled Corday's past clashes with *Soap Opera Weekly,* which he had allegedly banned from set visits after they dared critique *Days*—yet the magazine continued to cover the show anyway, further fueling Corday's resentment.

His response only reignited talk of his long-simmering tension with Reilly—an uneasy partnership marked by creative clashes and differing visions for what *Days* should be.

Former soap journalist Jamey Giddens once reflected on Reilly's impact in an article for Daytime Confidential.

"I firmly believe that *Days of Our Lives* would have been cancelled right along with *Another World* in the late '90s without the juggernaut ratings brought on by Reilly's storylines. Corday seems to refuse to acknowledge what this man brought to his show. Vivian, Carly, Kate, Sami—we love these characters because of what Reilly wrote for them."

Those whispers became reality. On June 2, 2003, *Variety* broke the news that NBC had officially struck a deal to have Reilly oversee both soaps. The agreement, brokered by NBC Senior VP of Daytime Sheraton Kalouria, was part of a broader renewal deal for *Days* through May 2009. Kalouria, who had just re-upped for another three years as head of daytime, called Reilly "the right guy to be the creative leader overseeing the next wave of stories for *Days*."

He added, "We saw in Jim someone who had a proven track record, and we wanted to bring him back."

Even Corday publicly played along. "I had qualms about it at first only because it's a huge task to write five shows a week, and now you're asking him to write ten," he told *Variety.* "But Jim has the appetite and the skills, so away we go."

Years later, however, Corday's memoir *The Days of Our Lives,* told a different story. Referring to Jim's second stint at *Days:* "Unfortunately, the second time around, I was given no alternative. They said, 'Do it this way or we will take the show off.' They were overpowering at NBC."

The truth was simple. Jim Reilly was now writing two soaps at once, and only time would tell if he could handle both.

CHAPTER FIFTEEN — *Behind the Scenes*

Associate head writer Marlene McPherson told us an interesting fact about *Passions* creator Jim Reilly. "He always claimed when he was doing his residency after medical school that he delivered a two-headed baby. My daughter interviewed him for a school project, and he still laid claim to that story."

That sense of the unbelievable extended beyond his writing. It seeped into the show's culture. On set, ask any cast member, and they will tell you there was no shortage of pranks behind the scenes. For all of its over-the-top storylines, the energy behind the cameras was just as wild. The cast became notorious for inside jokes and antics that helped long shoot days go by faster.

When asked who the biggest troublemakers were, Jade Harlow, who played Jessica Bennett, did not hesitate. "The boys... all the boys. I mean, I'll name names—Jesse, number one, Galen, James. Travis was in that mix, but the ones that hazed me were in that particular order."

She laughed as she recalled one of her most vivid memories. "I'll give you a perfect example. We were shooting some Crane wedding, and there was a procession coming out of the church. The residents of Harmony were lined up as the bride and groom passed. They gave us all bird seed—a big sack of it—and we were supposed to toss it when the bride and groom came by, like, 'Yay!' When we did the first take, I got pelted *hard* with bird seed. I'm looking around like, how did that happen? And Jesse's right across from me, and I knew it was him. So when they came back around, I'm like, I got this, I got you, it's on. I made a big sweaty snowball of bird seed and had every intention of getting him right in the face with it. I accidentally hit Andrea Evans in the eye and got in trouble. But nobody knew who started it, and I wasn't going to throw him under the bus."

Hookups on set added another layer of chaos, something the cast rarely talked about publicly. Natalie Zea spilled that several members of the "Scooby-Doo crew"—the show's younger set—were hooking up with each other. While most were tight-lipped about specific names, soap magazines had already covered that Jesse Metcalfe and Taylor Anne Mountz dated briefly during her tenure on the show.

Jade Harlow revealed during her interview on *The Real ShowCast*, "Everybody dated everybody. I'm pretty sure every Miguel dated every Kay in real life, at least while I was there."

She admitted that Bruce Michael Hall, who played Reese, was her first-ever boyfriend. "I actually lost my virginity to him, and then we dated for like a year. You know how when you lose your virginity and they're not a virgin, but you are, and you don't want to be just another notch on their belt? I talked Bruce into getting matching wedding ring tattoos, and then shortly thereafter we amicably broke up. But we both still carry the mark."

She showed her hand before continuing, "I'm on my third session of tattoo removal, which hurts a lot more than getting it done." She joked, "It's a great way to tell Bruce and Seth apart," referring to the twin brothers who both played Reese. Before joining *Passions,* Bruce and Seth Hall were known in the late 1990s for a string of successful modeling campaigns. They booked fitness work, commercial shoots, and even several underwear ads that highlighted their hard abs and athletic build. Fans who only knew Reese as Harmony's earnest science nerd would never guess that the twins once modeled in low-rise briefs before trading it all in for button-down shirts, khakis, and thick glasses to play him.

The characters of Jessica and Reese started dating on the show. When Bruce left, his twin brother Seth Hall took over the role. Jade remembered how awkward that was. "I had to kiss my former boyfriend's twin brother. That was odd. I was like, wow, y'all are really going to have us do this? Okay, alright."

Not everyone was part of the shenanigans. Chrystee Pharris made sure we knew she wasn't involved, admitting she was older than the "Scooby-Doo crew"—25 playing 16.

Backstage chaos wasn't reserved just to the teen crew. James Hyde recalled, "The funniest thing was when I finished a scene on a Friday and everybody was pissed because we had a long day." He continued, "I walked off [stage] and Galen was waiting for me with baby powder and—boom." Hyde remembered thinking he hoped that was the last take of the day.

Galen Gering then explained how angry everyone was because they had first drenched Hyde in body lotion to make the baby powder really stick. "The stage manager was like, 'Hold on. Okay, James, come back.' And he hadn't seen him, and James was just completely destroyed. They were like, 'Oh my god, you freaking idiots.' They hated us."

Lindsay Hartley told us that Eric Martsolf was the funniest person she knows, and that she always laughs around him. It's not hard to see why, as he admitted he may or may not have run across the set in his underwear belting out "The Circle of Life."

Now a married couple, Natalie Zea and Travis Schuldt humorously reflected on their days on set in a joint interview. Zea recalled, "Those of us who went to theatre school would ask, 'What's our motivation?' and they'd say, 'Thursday,' because that was the day the checks came out." Both laughed. "We'd be like, yeah, but what's my motivation—why am I going from here to there, what's the motive?… 'Thursday. Three, two, one!'" They cracked up at the memory.

Travis also recalled, "Eva Tamargo Lemus (who played Pilar Lopez-Fitzgerald) used to have huge Halloween parties with the whole cast, and we'd all get dressed up and have fun. Juliet (Tabitha Lenox) did a Halloween party too. We were family."

Natalie added, "I had a good friend of mine living with me at the time from New York. She came out with me to help me get set up, so when we had social things I told her to come along and be my wingman. After the first couple of times she was like, 'How do y'all get any work done?'" Referring, of course, to the stunningly gorgeous cast.

Natalie joked how she wasn't single at the time, very much in a relationship. She and Travis wouldn't start dating—and later marry—until after leaving the show.

It is these moments—between the laughter, the absurdity, and the family-like chaos—you could see the tight bond that the entire cast shared. As they looked at photos from the parties they' had thrown and reminisced, it was clear the show's magic was not just in the scripts or the special effects. It was in the people, the pranks, and the joy of creating something they had no idea would be remembered and cherished. Those memories are a snapshot of a young, fearless cast making magic together.

CHAPTER SIXTEEN — *Mind Behind the Curtain*

Series creator James E. Reilly once confessed that he was always thinking about *Passions*. Miles away from the Los Angeles studio, living quietly in his mock-Tudor estates along the Atlantic coast, he described how inspiration followed him everywhere. "If I walk down the street and meet people, I wonder if they look like someone on *Passions!* Everything can be a story point," he told *Soap Opera Weekly*. "If I'm watching television or the news, something will strike me and I'll wonder, will that fit in?"

In that same interview, Jim reflected on why people tune into stories like his. "I think people watch soaps for the same reason the *Iliad* and *Odyssey* were memorized and told over nights and nights of storytelling thousands of years ago. These stories were told to entertain the audience and get them involved in characters' lives. People wanted to be entertained by stories 3,000 years ago, they want to be entertained by stories today, and they'll want to be entertained by stories 2,000 years from now."

It was one of the few times Jim allowed anyone to glimpse the scale of his thinking in an interview, which he rarely did. He wasn't just writing a soap opera. He was building a modern mythology.

Darrell Ray Thomas, who served as an associate head writer alongside Marlene McPherson throughout *Passions'* entire run, was Jim's protégé. "When I first met Jim, I was an intern at *Days of Our Lives*," he recalled. "Part of my school project was to have an interview with him, and one of the first questions I asked was, 'What's it like?

You write it, and then you turn it over, and then you see it on television, what's that like?' He told me how wonderful it is to see what's in his head come to life. And I know that on *Passions*, his vision was brought to life better than ever before. On the production side, Lisa and Richard, the things they did were unbelievable."

Thomas was promoted to the writing staff during his time at *Days* and later followed Jim to *Passions*. He remembered, "There was a huge fight between *Days* and *Passions* and 'Don't take our people.' I was the first one that went over, and even though I'd given my resignation and there'd been enough time, I was kind of like a guinea pig. Is this going to be the fight? Who can't go?"

He said working for Jim was an honor. "Everything came from Jim." Remembering wild storylines like the prom boat disaster, Thomas smiled. "I'd walk into the studio where they had that water tank, and it was so big and so intimidating, and these actors were so committed. They were in there giving their best to make everything come to life, and Jim was always in awe of that."

Reflecting on Jim's creative courage, he added, "He kept pushing the boundaries, and I know that was something very important to him. He wanted to show as much of America as we could. There was a lot of diversity in the show that you didn't see anywhere else, not just in daytime, anywhere on television. And he really liked to push the envelope, to show what America was ready for. When the network said, 'Oh, you can't do that,' he'd say, 'Well, we're going to do it anyway.' That was his attitude. He fought for what he believed in, and he fought for putting out there what we are and what people have fought for. He was a great advocate for that, besides being, I think, a genius."

Thomas also spoke of Jim's mind and how encyclopedic it was. "You know he was a doctor," he reminds us. "He was so well read. He knew everything. I majored in English and literature, and you could see the Shakespearean and Greek stuff, those ties coming out. He loved pop culture too, and we threw a lot of that at the screen. It was brilliant, the way he could pick the exact right characters to put into those homages to the movies. He made connections people don't usually make. I don't know where that comes from. It's almost like a mystical, cosmic consciousness type of thing."

Soap journalist Connie Passaicqua Hayman once wrote, "My favorite Reilly story, which I must have written about a dozen times, was Underground France on *Days*. That story, where John was going to have his head cut off in the guillotine, just cracked me up. It was so elaborate, so nuts. But nutsy in a fun way, and Jim did it because he knew French history! Jim was very well read, very up on the events of the day, very knowledgeable on many academic subjects. When he created Hecuba, the character Robin Strasser so wonderfully played on *Passions*, he had me running to the bookstore for a copy of the *Iliad*."

On-screen, that cosmic consciousness found its voice in moments both absurd and transcendent. In an episode, Dr. Eve Russell, dressed in surgical scrubs, stands over Tabitha Lennox, who is strapped to a table as if for an autopsy. "It is a known fact that witches feel pain," Eve says to the audience, breaking the fourth wall. "They scream when being burned at the stake, when being touched by a crucifix, or when melting, as in the case of the Wicked Witch of the West. The question then becomes, how much pain do they feel?"

Tabitha squints and deadpans, "What the hell kind of day spa is this?"

Eve raises a small handsaw and flicks the blade. "The perfect pitch for sawing a witch."

The scene encapsulated everything that made *Passions* singular: dark humor, high camp, and a wink to the audience that somehow made the ridiculous feel profound.

Actress Tracey Ross, who played Dr. Eve Russell, often compared her character to the Professor on *Gilligan's Island*. "If there's a dead body, I'm the coroner. If someone has a heart attack, I'm a cardiologist. If we'd had a dog, I'd have been the vet," she laughed.

"You have to have that person who knows everything and brings the reasonable explanation for what's going on. That's what Eve did."

She added, "Eve also served another purpose. You'd have the gorgeous guy, and there were so many of them lying in the hospital bed, chest bare, covers never pulled up, so you can see their six and eight packs. My job was to go in, check him, come back out, close the curtain, and say nothing while the family waited for news. After three commercial breaks, or maybe the next day, I'd finally say one of two lines. 'Only love can save him now,' or, 'All we can do is pray.'" She laughed again.

Moments like these reflected Reilly's ability to fold satire into sincerity. His shows were outrageous but never empty. Behind the witches, doll boys, and portals to hell was a man who saw storytelling as sacred, who believed entertainment could be both ridiculous and revealing.

Reilly's cosmic imagination didn't stop at absurdity and satire; it extended into the realm of human emotion, where love, desire, and heartbreak were as fantastical and carefully orchestrated as any other plot he conceived.

His characters, Sheridan and Luis, were star-crossed lovers, a term coined by William Shakespeare to describe *Romeo and Juliet* — two souls bound by love yet divided by fate. Their love was repeatedly doomed by forces beyond their control, including circumstance, ill-fated destiny, and external obstacles. Across past lives, they appeared as Cleopatra and Marc Antony, passengers on the Titanic, and swashbucklers in a *Pirates of the Caribbean* homage, among others. In every incarnation, even this one, their love ended in heartbreak, with Tabitha never far behind. These storylines showcased Jim's ability to blend romance, tragedy, and fantasy, turning doomed love into modern soap mythology.

He may have hidden from the public eye, but his fingerprints covered every inch of *Passions*. He wrote like a novelist, thought like a theologian, and dreamed like a showman. To those who worked beside him, he wasn't an enigma to be solved. He was a universe to be translated.

Jim's stories were steeped in contradictions: faith and temptation, secrecy and revelation, punishment and grace. His Catholic imagination gave him a moral language for desire, and his empathy gave him the courage to write it. Whether by instinct or lived experience, he understood the pain of those who walk between worlds—the devout and the damned, the seen and the hidden.

James E. Reilly was, and remains, the soul of *Passions*: a recluse who never stopped writing, a doctor who prescribed dreams, and a man who saw divinity in melodrama.

CHAPTER SEVENTEEN — *Faith in Harmony*

By the end of 2003, *Passions* was wilder than ever on screen, but behind the scenes, real life sometimes took priority over spectacle. Among the year's most surprising cast changes was the departure of Deanna Wright. She had stepped into the role of Kay Bennett following Gina Marie May's temporary stint after Taylor Anne Mountz's exit. For three years, fans had embraced Deanna's version of Kay — headstrong, flawed, impulsive — but she later revealed that she felt a personal calling to walk away.

She explained that her character's choices were often at odds with her Christian convictions, and that it had been placed on her heart to move on.

Chrystee Pharris, who played Simone Russell, recalled a moment between them that would deepen their bond.

"I'll never forget, I had just gotten on the show," Chrystee said. "My faith is strong, and one day Deanna had a breakdown. She was in the corner crying. I felt the Lord telling me to go pray with her. I was like, 'I can't do that, I'll get fired for bringing this whole Christian thing to set.' But the feeling was so strong that I finally went over, put my hand on her back, and started praying."

A few weeks later, Chrystee was called into casting director Jackie Briskey's office.

"I thought I was in trouble," Chrystee laughed, remembering that she had just joined the show. "When I went to her office, she said,

'Chrystee, Deanna's uncle passed away.' It was tragic how he passed. 'They want you there when they tell her.' I was shocked. I said, 'Me? I just got here.'"

Jackie explained that Deanna had told her parents about the prayer that day, and they wanted Chrystee by her side. What followed was one of those moments that reveal a person's true heart.

"When they told her, she just cried," Chrystee said softly, her voice catching with emotion as she remembered the day. "All I could do was be there for her. It was such a special moment, because if I hadn't listened to that voice and gone over to her, we never would have shared that experience, and who knows how she would have handled it. There were so many moments like that on set that I'll never, ever forget."

Amid the chaos, it was a quiet moment that reminded everyone *Passions* wasn't just a workplace or a show—it was a family.

After Deanna's departure, the role of Kay Bennett was recast with newcomer Heidi Mueller, a fresh face who had first caught NBC's attention on the reality show *Who Wants to Marry My Dad*? Though some fans were skeptical of the transition, Heidi's warmth and openness quickly won audiences over. Fresh and eager to learn, she had a front-row seat to a masterclass every day, performing alongside the legendary Juliet Mills. She would go on to play Kay for the remainder of the show's run.

Chrystee's friendship with Deanna endured long after both women left Harmony, a testament to the unseen bonds that often outlasted the show itself. On a show defined by miracles, curses, and resurrections, sometimes the most powerful faith was not written into a script but lived quietly between takes.

As *Passions* moved into its next chapter, that same spirit of love, loyalty, and loss rippled through the cast and stories alike, blurring the line between fiction and real life.

CHAPTER EIGHTEEN — *Real Love and Loss*

While *Passions* had no shortage of characters pining for love on screen, off screen, love was in the air too. Executive producer Lisa Hesser, now Lisa de Cazotte, was living her fairy tale with her husband, French filmmaker Antoine de Cazotte, whom she met on the first day of taping *Passions* in Paris. They were celebrating their first year of marriage.

In a reunion after the show ended, McKenzie Westmore, who was a part of the Paris shoot recalled, "I remember the two of them meeting, it was magic from the start, and it was so beautiful to watch as an outside perspective on the two of them meeting."

"They were madly in love. She was so happy," soap journalist Connie Hyman remembered of the two.

After six months of dating, Justin Hartley and Lindsay Korman became engaged, marrying on May 1, 2004, in a small ceremony. Just two months later, on July 3, 2004, they welcomed their daughter, Isabella Justice.

Reflecting on their relationship, Lindsay shared, "Justin is amazing. I'm really grateful he's in my life, and we have a beautiful daughter from it. *Passions* was such a huge part of my life."

Though the couple would quietly and amicably separate in 2012, Lindsay has continued to speak with warmth and respect for him in the years since. On social media, she wrote, "I appreciate my ex-husband Justin for not only being an exemplification of a solid man, but for being my dear friend and devoted father to our daughter. Simply put; for being family."

Tracey Ross and Ben Masters were also finally openly dating. Tracey recalled, "It was a secret at first, but we didn't keep it a secret, we just didn't say anything about it because in the beginning you don't know where it's going or how long it's going. You don't want to tell people you're dating somebody that you work with and then two weeks later it's over, it's awkward. You could see that we'd been growing closer and closer, but I think it probably just looked like we were really close friends. And yeah, then I don't know exactly, I think it was probably at least a year before we actually just made it clear that we were together."

On the show, Eve's secrets were starting to catch up to her, and by that point Liz, Eve's adoptive sister, was giving her hell. Liz even went as far as to bring their Aunt Irma out of the nursing home in a guest-starring role that had television legend Marla Gibbs reprising the part of the slick-talking aunt who couldn't stand Eve and her, as Aunt Irma would put it, slutty ways, calling her a whore and a tramp every second she could.

Marla Gibbs remembered, "Aunt Irma picked up a lot of fans, and I couldn't believe it, because Aunt Irma is crazy," she laughed. "I think all of it was fun, asking me to be deranged and have my hair all crazy, that was fun."

Tracey Ross admitted she was fangirling on set having Marla Gibbs there, having grown up a fan of hers. She said she felt honored, and that Marla was so warm.

These storylines brought the characters of Eve and Julian closer, and their real-life chemistry shined through their scenes, with the fan base suddenly rooting for the two to be together in what they lovingly called "Evian."

Tracey Ross recalled, "Julian was a terrible person—funny as heck, but terrible. Watching him change for the love of Eve, wanting to protect her and do something for someone besides himself, was beautiful. Eve, lacking any way to protect herself, leaned on him, and their scenes created a beautiful duet." Yet as love blossomed around the set, life sometimes reminded everyone of its fragility.

Just as love comes, loss can come just as easily. From the show's premiere in 1999, Alistair Crane was heard but rarely seen. Like Charlie from *Charlie's Angels*, his presence was known through his voice, provided by Alan Oppenheimer, while his body was portrayed by Bill Dempsey. He remained a central, enigmatic figure until September 2004, when David Bailey was cast and finally revealed Alistair's face. Tragically, only 31 episodes into the role, Bailey drowned in a pool accident at his Los Angeles home at the age of 71. Executive producer Lisa de Cazotte released a statement reflecting on his passing. "It is with great sadness that we learned of the sudden passing of David Bailey. He was a man of great compassion and kindness as well as an extraordinary actor."

"David Bailey made an immediate and indelible impression in his role as patriarch of the Crane family on *Passions*," NBC Universal Television's Senior Vice President of Daytime, Sheraton Kalouria, added at the time.

Just as love and devotion shaped lives on set, the sudden passing of David Bailey reminded everyone that loss could strike unexpectedly, leaving a profound impact both on screen and in the hearts of those who brought the show to life.

CHAPTER NINETEEN— *Growing Pains*

By late 2004, a quiet shift was underway in Harmony. The show wasn't collapsing — but it was changing. Familiar faces had left, new ones arrived, and the show settled into a different rhythm. Some of the changes were driven by contracts, others by creative decisions, but with the relentless pace of daytime production, adaptation was the only option.

Dana Sparks exited as Grace Bennett, her character moving to Italy with David (Justin Carroll) and her supposed son, John (Jack Krizmanich). Molly Stanton soon followed, ending her run as Charity. Her final episode featured a montage of Charity's many supernatural adventures — a fitting farewell for a character who had embodied the show's wildest magic, both as Charity and Zombie Charity. Juliet Mills fondly recalled, "She was always drenched in water, buried in the snow, in the mud, falling into the sea. They put that girl through hell!"

After leaving *Passions*, Stanton transitioned into primetime, starring in *Twins* with Sara Gilbert and Melanie Griffith and later *Do Not Disturb* with Jerry O'Connell and Niecy Nash. Today, she is an aesthetician and proud owner of Sage Lane Skincare.

Like Molly Stanton, Jesse Metcalfe left Harmony for primetime success, focusing on his *Desperate Housewives* role that he initially juggled with *Passions*. He would later headline the film *John Tucker Must Die* with Brittany Snow, Ashanti, Sophia Bush, and Jenny

McCarthy, appear in the *Dallas* revival, and become a familiar face on the Hallmark Channel.

As its young stars flourished elsewhere, *Passions* struggled in the ratings, often ranking last among the remaining daytime soaps after the cancellation of *Port Charles*. Occasionally, it edged out *Guiding Light*, but its strongest following remained among younger viewers. NBC leaned into that demographic with the character of Jessica Bennett, now played by Danica Stewart. The show partnered with Avon's "mark." cosmetics line in a rare instance of daytime product integration, both in commercials and on-screen storylines.

Meanwhile, after contract disputes led to Chrystee Pharris' departure, the show welcomed Cathy Janean Doe as Simone. *Passions* made daytime history as the first soap to depict two women in bed together, when Simone was revealed to be in a secret relationship with Rae (Jossara Jinaro). Jinaro, remembered fondly by fans, passed away from cancer in 2022 at the age of 48.

New faces continued to populate Harmony. Silvana Arias joined as Paloma Lopez-Fitzgerald, the youngest sibling in the Lopez-Fitzgerald family. Her arrival coincided with major story revelations as Martin Fitzgerald (Richard Steinmetz), Katherine Crane (Leigh Taylor-Young), and her sister Rachel Barrett (Sharon Wyatt) were all revealed to be alive. Around the same time, Alistair Crane was recast with John Reilly, whose more theatrical and mustache-twirling performance brought a new take to the show's most notorious villain.

Daphnee Duplaix also joined the cast as Valerie Davis, a Crane Industries employee. She had briefly appeared in 1999 as Buffy, one of Gwen's sorority sisters, a bit part most fans never connected to her later role. Her reappearance seemed small at first, but it would eventually lead her into one of the most unexpected and unforgettable storylines in the history of the show.

As *Passions* adjusted its cast and tone, the magical mayhem that once defined the show took a temporary backseat. Tabitha became more of a mentor figure to Kay, observing Harmony's drama from her kitchen's enchanted bowl. The supernatural still flickered, most notably through baby Endora's thought bubbles, but the emphasis had shifted.

By 2005, another transition came behind the scenes. Sheraton Kalouria departed NBC Daytime from his executive role, marking yet another turning point during one of Passions' most transformative years.

With so many transitions both in front of and behind the camera, *Passions* entered its middle years with a different heartbeat — steadier, quieter, but still unmistakably its own.

CHAPTER TWENTY — *Disaster and Ecstasy*

In an attempt to revive *Passions,* the show launched one of its most ambitious storylines yet: the "Passions Disaster." When Tabitha and Endora's magical powers accidentally crossed beams, they triggered a massive earthquake and a subsequent tsunami that ripped through Harmony, shaking the show to its core.

NBC went all out for the event, even hosting a red-carpet screening at Universal Studios Hollywood. Cast members mingled with fans who showed up in droves, a clear reminder of how much passion still burned for the daytime drama.

Eric Martsolf (Ethan) remembered the tsunami well. "I remember being wet for a long time. I remember going to the commissary and getting my cheeseburger and sitting down and just itching because we weren't allowed to change our clothes. They're like, 'Eric, why don't you just stay in those jeans and that underwear for the next eight hours, soaking wet?' And I was like, okay, yeah, because we don't want to change." He laughs. "But that being said, it was amazing. We had homes that were submerged underwater. We had dudes in scuba gear filming us. We had a wave machine that would propel Lindsay and I down a stretch of water. It was amazing. It was like we were filming Jaws or something. They built an ocean on the set."

He added, "I just constantly remember being surprised at the amount of commitment, money, people, and time that they put into these scenes. Even though the material may have been silly at times, we took it seriously because we knew the manpower that was needed. They worked really hard."

Around this time, new characters like Noah Bennett (Dylan Fergus) and Fancy Crane (Emily Harper) were introduced to bring fresh energy to the canvas. Whitney gave birth to her son, Miles, terrified she had given birth to her brother's child—a fear that sent her checking into a convent, though it would later be revealed that the two weren't related.

Christopher Maleki, who played Spike, recalled those wild years opposite Danica Stewart's Jessica Bennett, where his character embodied the ultimate bad boy of Harmony. "Initially I came on for three episodes. I was the club owner, no name. They said depending on how well the character does will determine how long he lasts. I did a couple hundred episodes, of course, and after three shows they were like, 'Chris, we're going to shop for you now,'" he remembered.

Maleki also recalled his first scene with Rodney Van Johnson (T.C.). "I did a scene with Rodney, and I had just met him. They told me, 'Rodney gets very physical, so we wanted to put some pads on you.' I said, 'No, no, it's cool. He's just gonna grab me.' And they said, 'Oh... you've never worked with Rodney before? Because he gets so into it.'

"So we get in there for the scene, which involved his daughter Simone, and I apparently hit her in the head with a club. I come over to the house, the director is giving us direction, and I look over at Rodney—he's glaring at me, literally just wants to kill me. I kind of taunt him a little, even though we haven't started shooting yet. I knew trouble was coming.

"He got so into it, he threw me toward the table. I understand why they told me to wear pads—he threw me so hard my arm got skinned and pushed back. The scene continued. Then the police in the scene come to separate us, and I, to fill the moment, pretend like I'm trying to punch him. When it was over, they said cut, beautiful, moving on.

"And the next thing I hear is him yelling, 'Don't you ever throw a punch at me without blocking it!' He said it loud so everyone could hear, and I felt completely disrespected. I had just gotten on the show, but I had to sound off: 'Hey man, pain is temporary, film's forever, I get it, but look at me. You hear me complaining? I skinned my arm.'

"They ended up calling me up to the production office to see if everything was okay. It was just the heat of the moment, you know? I love the guy, but that was my first time working with him."

Rodney's character T.C. was often revved up, and Rodney didn't like his character becoming the angry Black man, a direction he found difficult. He shared, "I literally had to detox every day after working, because the emotions were so high. I had to go kick butt, be angry, scream, and get into that whole mode every day. Loved the work, but it was very, very hard to come down from. I live seven minutes from the studio, but going home it would take an hour and a half because I would literally have to detox. I had to drive somewhere and just sit and relax because I didn't want to take all that anger home to my new son.

"That was probably the toughest part of being T.C.—that anger management stuff. And that's one of the things I wish they had dealt with on the show. Anger management, how you deal with it and how you cope."

His character would eventually have a stroke. Rodney shared how his Uncle Dwayne had one and survived for thirteen years, and he was able to channel that. As an actor, he knew his days were numbered. He was preparing to be written off and remembers it as a somber time.

Despite the intensity behind the scenes, the show continued to push creative boundaries and was still able to deliver some of its most memorable moments on screen.

On Friday, January 27, 2006, *Passions* went Bollywood.

In the storyline, Gwen grew increasingly paranoid that Theresa was trying to lure Ethan away from her. Convinced a romantic

85

getaway would keep them united, she persuaded Ethan to travel to India so they could renew their vows far away from Theresa's influence.

But as Gwen fantasized about the perfect ceremony, her daydream took a wildly musical turn—transforming the scene into a full-blown Bollywood extravaganza, complete with an ensemble of desi background dancers, elaborate costumes, and a colorful dance number set around the symbolic Tree of Life.

Just as Gwen and Ethan's imagined happiness reached its peak, Theresa appeared in a far more minimalist version of a sari, with a black veil and her trademark smirk. Gwen's fantasy instantly spiraled into her nightmare.

Eric Martsolf recalled, "It was Gwen's nightmare, and I'll never forget walking onto that set, thinking to myself, Spielberg needs to see this. I mean, this is cool. I don't know what *Close Encounters* looked like, but this is amazing. And we did it, and they committed to it, and I've never been on a set that beautiful since. It was amazing." He added, "NBC really did get behind *Passions*, and they threw some dollars and some commitment and some energy into that show. I think that's what the fans really appreciated, because they were transported into other worlds. Even if it was just for a dream sequence, they would do a giant blockbuster Bollywood nightmare, and that's amazing. You don't see that today in soap operas, so I commend them for that."

The sequence was both hilarious and visually stunning, and it paid off. The moment earned the show's music department another Daytime Emmy Award, this time for Outstanding Original Song for "Love Is Ecstasy," composed by John Henry Kreitler and Wes Boatman.

Passions found itself back in the mainstream conversation when it was featured on VH1's *Best Week Ever,* with Eric and Liza making an appearance. The weekly pop-culture series was known for its sharp humor and fast-paced recaps of celebrity gossip, television, and internet moments that defined each week. Its inclusion of *Passions* was a reminder that, even years into its run, the show could still capture attention beyond the soap world and remain part of the larger cultural conversation.

CHAPTER TWENTY-ONE — *Shifting Storylines*

By 2006, after ratings began to slip again at *Days of Our Lives*, NBC asked Jim Reilly to return his focus exclusively to *Passions*. Over the years, Reilly had earned a reputation for crafting some of daytime television's most memorable exits, moments that were as dramatic behind the scenes as they were on screen.

Some actors found themselves at the center of these storylines more than once. Thaao Penghlis, who had played Tony Dimera and his look-alike counterpart Andre Dimera off and on on *Days of Our Lives* since 1981, recalled the peculiar rhythm of his characters' fates. In an interview with *SheKnows' Soaps*, he explained that word had gotten back to Jim Reilly that he had negatively critiqued the writing. Soon after, Penghlis found himself in the path of spectacular exits.

"It was never, you know, I go upstairs and disappear, or I died from an overdose," he said. "No, the lion, the tiger attacked me. I fell on the spike of a thing. I thought, 'Oh, wait a minute. The spike going through my heart. That's what happened to Dracula. Is that how he saw me?'"

Fans of the sitcom *Friends* may remember the infamous episode "The One Where Dr. Ramoray Dies," in which Joey's *Days of Our Lives* character, Dr. Drake Ramoray, meets a swift and memorable end by falling down an elevator shaft after boasting in a magazine interview that he writes his own lines. Reilly appeared as himself in the episode, a cameo appearance in which he orchestrates the demise with a playful wink at the high-stakes drama he was accustomed to creating on daytime television.

Back in Harmony, the production team had to adapt to real-life circumstances, which occasionally required shifts in storylines. A few years earlier during the infamous "pit" storyline, a pregnancy plot collided with a personal loss, creating tension on set. McKenzie Westmore (Sheridan) miscarried in real life. In interviews, she has spoken openly about miscarrying and then returning to film Sheridan's birth scenes that were already written into the storyline. It was the kind of story that made fans tune in each day to watch Beth's plan to pass baby Marty off as her own, but it was just as dramatic off-screen.

Her struggles didn't stop there. During *Passions*, according to McKenzie, she battled an eating disorder, alleging her agent said, "You're looking fat next to the other girls. You have to lose weight."

Her version of events sometimes sits uneasily beside other memories from the same period. Long before she ever set foot on the *Passions* set, she was chasing the image she thought the business wanted. In a discussion with *Passions Podcast* after her time on the show, McKenzie explained, "I knew it was a soap, I knew there was like sexy daytime kind of stuff, and I'm like, well, I'm sure they don't want some flat-chested chick, and you know, early 2000s, that was not the thing. We're coming out of the Pamela Anderson era, so I kept stuffing my bra. I remember going to my mom, and I was like, I'm just not comfortable with this right now, and she was like, 'if you want to go do something about it, I support you,' so I went and got breast implants." While it wasn't a studio request or network suggestion, the 19-year-old went through with it and auditioned for the role of Gwen. Producers thought she fit the role of Sheridan better, which was meant to be older, and she was cast.

While other cast members would later describe Harmony as close-knit and supportive, like a family, McKenzie did an interview with *SheKnows Soaps*, with a headline calling the on-set culture at *Passions* "toxic." She shared, "I was constantly starving myself, constantly dieting, constantly dehydrating myself, taking laxatives, taking speed pills — not speed itself, but pills to rev me up" in the interview, describing the self-infliction. These accounts reflect McKenzie's personal experiences as she has described them in multiple interviews.

When a severe ear infection led to vertigo, forcing her to wear a patch, daytime television shuffled and adapted to the changes. A temporary Sheridan was brought on so filming could continue while McKenzie was unavailable. On set, production moved quickly to bring on Shannon Sturges, stepping in during late May 2005 while McKenzie recovered.

Production was concerned for McKenzie when she would later be hospitalized. Things behind the scenes were unclear, and pivots needed to be made. She shared in her own words in that interview, "NBC threatened a lawsuit if I didn't come back. I had to leave the hospital and go back to work. I had to promise the hospital in getting released that I would go to therapy several times a week — and I did it."

If past choices were any guide, Reilly's knack for creative pivots was never far from mind. The story soon shifted to the pairing of Luis and Fancy. For viewers who had shipped Sheridan and Luis from the beginning, it felt like the goalposts had moved yet again for the star-crossed lovers, never able to truly live in love across their many past lives, including this one. Newer fans, unaware of the couple's history, fell for the Fancy and Luis pairing. It wouldn't be long before longtime fans and newer fans clashed on message boards over who Luis should end up with.

Elsewhere in Harmony, actors remembered laughter and long shooting days. In an interview with *Soap Opera Digest* at the time, Emily Harper, who played Fancy Crane, shared, "He's [Galen Gering] so much fun to work with. It's been crazy since Fancy and Luis paired up - from chasing Beth and Marty, to going through training and becoming a cop. Now we've got Luis' execution and the wedding. A lot has gone on."

In the same interview, Emily spoke on how close she and Heidi Mueller (Kay) were and how the cast would get together for birthdays. She added, "It's not only cast members. I just went out with our stage manager, Cherie Wall. We're a tight-knit family over here. I can't stress how lucky we are. My co-workers are such good people and the show has a zany quality which allows us to laugh and have fun together."

In July 2006, McKenzie experienced joy with the birth of her son, Maddox Volpone. Kam Heskin briefly stepped in as Sheridan while McKenzie was on maternity leave. Years later, McKenzie would reflect on the show, "Mentally, it was not the best environment." In the show's final year, Heskin was called back once more to step into Sheridan's heels—because, in Harmony, the drama never took a day off.

In recent interviews, McKenzie shares that following the show she underwent reconstructive procedures after dealing with bad filler treatments. She'd launch Westmore Beauty as the founder and on-air spokesperson—a brand built on the promise of a natural finish.

While temporary recasts, personal struggles, and unexpected crises tested production, fans at home remained blissfully unaware. For them, Harmony existed as a fully realized world of magic, romance, and intrigue, untouched by the challenges faced on set, and soon, reruns.

CHAPTER TWENTY-TWO — *Soundtrack of Harmony*

Even as *Passions* continued its new weekday broadcasts on NBC, fans who had missed the early years or simply wanted to relive the magic of Harmony got a surprise when the Sci-Fi Channel, now SyFy, began airing reruns of the soap. The network had already seen success reviving the 1960s gothic soap *Dark Shadows* and hoped *Passions'* cult audience would tune in as well. For fans, seeing those early episodes again wasn't just a trip down memory lane—it was a return to the wild, irreverent Harmony that had first captured their imaginations.

While the episodes were largely identical to the original NBC airings, one thing stood out: the songs. At a time when streaming was not yet common and most daytime soaps never had the chance to be rerun from the start, producers had never anticipated long-term song rights. Licensing popular songs was expensive, and soaps typically secured only short-term agreements covering their initial broadcasts. As a result, the reruns replaced the original songs with generic tracks that rarely matched the tone or energy of the original scenes, leaving emotional beats feeling flatter or unintentionally awkward.

For *Passions*—which targeted a younger, pop-savvy audience— the show, especially early in its run, leaned heavily on recognizable music to enhance both mood and humor. Fans still remember "Celebrity Skin" by Hole when Theresa is first introduced in the show's premiere; "Livin' La Vida Loca" by Ricky Martin as the Lopez-Fitzgeralds dance in the kitchen; "Dude (Looks Like a Lady)" by Aerosmith during a playful montage of Kay playing dress-up with

Timmy; and "Absolutely Fabulous" by Pet Shop Boys in Tabitha's daydream of becoming a famous author like Jackie Collins and having her photo taken, with Timmy as her agent of course. These songs defined the decade and helped make *Passions* feel alive, modern, and self-aware. Even hits from Backstreet Boys, Britney Spears, Madonna, and Brandy & Monica's 'The Boy Is Mine'— featured in the original broadcasts—were replaced by generic tracks in reruns.

When Canada's Super Channel followed suit, the same replacements persisted, though devoted collectors still treasure original NBC recordings with the true soundtrack intact. Episodes posted to YouTube, often sourced from the Sci-Fi and Super Channel reruns, feature these replacement tracks, leading to confusion among longtime viewers and jokes from new fans about the "terrible music," unaware that the original songs were lost to licensing restrictions.

But even as licensing restrictions muted some of Harmony's past, *Passions* kept music at the heart of its storytelling—often by bringing artists directly into the world of the show.

Leading the charge was McKenzie Westmore's now ex-husband, Keith "Seven" Volpone, who appeared on *Passions* with his band Seven and the Sun to perform "Walk With Me," the first single from their debut Atlantic album Back to the Innocence. The song underscored a summer-long storyline, and the band performed it uninterrupted during an episode. The exposure caught Atlantic Records by surprise, and to meet the strong demand from fans, the label moved up the album's release.

Following Seven and the Sun, the series welcomed a string of performers who appeared on *Passions* to perform their hits, including Grammy Award–winning artist Mýa with her single "My Love Is Like… Wo," and the Scissor Sisters, known for their theatrical blend of glam rock, pop, and dance-disco, performing "I Don't Feel Like Dancin'" and "Land of a Thousand Words." Even Jane French, the singer of the *Passions* theme song, released an album sold in the NBC Experience Store featuring the theme "Breathe." In a rare move for daytime television, the show even produced a full music video for the theme. French's second album, Euphoria, which included songs dedicated to the characters of Theresa and Ethan and Luis and Sheridan, was also available. Music wasn't just background; it gave viewers a heartbeat, a pulse for the drama and whimsy unfolding onscreen.

Through these musical moments, *Passions* blurred the line between daytime drama and pop-culture spectacle, giving its fans an experience that extended far beyond the television screen. The combination of magic, chaos, and music further cemented the show's impact, making Harmony a place where anything—on or off the screen—was possible.

From witchcraft to wedding bells, *Passions* always moved to its own rhythm—a soundtrack that, even in silence, fans can still hear. Even when the curtain fell, Harmony kept singing.

CHAPTER TWENTY-THREE — *Mystic Mischief*

In 2006, Tabitha's daughter, baby Endora, conjured up a mermaid from one of her storybooks. Her goal was simple. She wanted to break up Miguel and Kay's romance. Kay was already engaged to Fox, who was Endora's half-brother. From Endora's magic came Siren, a mermaid brought to life by actress Brandi Burkhardt. After rescuing Miguel from drowning, Siren instantly fell in love. She tried to curse him so that he would only love her. What followed was a desperate attempt by Kay to separate the two and win Miguel back.

The supernatural mischief didn't end there. Soon, a new character, the Demon Elf, appeared, played by Danny Woodburn. Emerging straight from Hell, he offered to help Kay find her sister Jessica, who had been buried alive in a crate by Spike. But his help came with a price. After manipulating Kay into granting him more power, he unleashed a small army of demons across Harmony, delighting in chaos while tormenting the town's residents. He appeared everywhere in wild costumes, mocking and manipulating everyone in sight.

Following the show's Emmy-winning musical numbers, including the 2003 *Chicago* parody 'I Ain't Sorry' and the previous year's Bollywood fantasy, "Love Is Ecstasy," the series produced what would become its final musical episode, an origin story for Tabitha. Filled with *Wicked*-inspired energy, the episode featured original songs "Spellbinding" and "Perfectly Frightful." It was a lavish, tongue-in-cheek tribute to the classic Broadway musical *Wicked*, brought to life through dazzling choreography and elaborate costume design.

Costume designer Diana Eden later recalled, "We had something like forty-five costumes made from scratch. We brought in extra people to the workroom, we had a hat maker, we had a dyer. It was crazy here for two and a half weeks, but we made it."

Composer and lyricist John Henry Kreitler admitted he had never actually seen *Wicked,* though it was high on his list. "I listened to the songs a couple of times to appreciate what they're about and the musical universe they're in," he explained. "Then I put them aside and never listened again. The last thing I want to do is write those songs. That's not what we're about at *Passions.* We do original work, either spoofs or homages. This is a beautifully done tribute to the style and substance of *Wicked.*"

Choreographer Lance McDonald, who had worked with the show before, was brought in again for the production. "They went first class all the way," he said. "I don't get excited about a lot of work, but I was excited about this. I think it's quite special."

The episode was directed by longtime *Passions* director Phideaux Xavier.

Looking back on his time on set, Colton Shires, who played Little Ethan, remembered how magical the production felt from a child's point of view, surrounded by song, dance, and special effects. "I was 2 years old when the show first came out. It's just a little mind-blowing fact for me, and 4 years later I'm on the show, *ugh,* how lucky was I to find myself in that position."

Remembering Colton, Eric Martsolf joked, "He's not so little anymore, is he? He's like six foot nine or something like that?" He further reflected, "What a nice kid. What a beautiful attention span that boy had for that kind of environment. He always looked me in the eye, which is hard to get kids to do that these days. Hell, I have kids and I can't even get them to look me in the eye half the time. Colton was always on his game, and he was there for me. He had tears in his eyes when they needed to be, and he was very, very present. Very good actor."

By then, the series seemed to have regained its footing. New characters like Esme Vanderheusen and her niece Viki were being introduced, keeping Harmony's mix of absurdity and danger alive. Melinda Sward joined the cast as the last Crane child to appear on screen as Pretty Crane. Eva Tamargo Lemus, who played Pilar, even welcomed her daughter Gabby Lemus on set to play a younger version of Pilar in a flashback scene after introducing a new character, Juanita, portrayed by Jill Remez.

As *New York Times* bestselling author Angie Thomas put it, "*Passions* was wild, funny, and fearless. It was one of those shows that did what no one else would even dare to try."

CHAPTER TWENTY-FOUR — *Breaking Boundaries*

Passions, never one to shy away from firsts, became the first daytime drama to stream full episodes online—a groundbreaking move for its time. While that May word came that the soap would be renewed for another year, it would come with significant budget cuts. $4–5 million had been slashed from the budget, layoffs loomed, and uncertainty hovered—a scary time for everyone.

That summer, *Passions* introduced its Vendetta storyline, which had taken several Harmony residents to Rome. One memorable storyline focused on Theresa chasing J.T. Cornell (yours truly) through the streets of Rome, desperate to get proof that Gwen and Rebecca had exposed Ethan's paternity to the tabloids, hoping to win him back. In the now-infamous mid-chase scene, Theresa paused to deliver a lengthier-than-usual recap and monologue, catching viewers up before continuing her pursuit—a humorous moment still highlighted by fans.

I was also the one to show Chad Harris his birth certificate, revealing he was Liz's son, not Eve's (and since Liz was Eve's *adopted* sister, it meant Chad and Whitney weren't related). Of course, Chad and Whitney, relieved to learn they weren't siblings, would eventually marry. As they struggled to cut into the wedding cake, I tumbled out completely cooked—an incident that still haunts me.

By January 2007, things were looking grim. NBC announced plans to expand *The Today Show* from three to four hours on weekdays. Fronted by Matt Lauer, Meredith Vieira, Ann Curry, and

Al Roker, the long-running morning show was a proven moneymaker. At that winter's Television Critics Association press event, NBC confirmed the expansion.

The "super-sized" version of *Today* would leave affiliates with one less day slot, meaning NBC planned to cancel *Passions*, though not immediately. The show's contract ran until June, but with *Today's* new hour set to debut in the fall, NBC negotiated with the cast and crew to extend *Passions* through August 2007.

On screen, unbeknownst to Whitney, Chad had been secretly involved in a sexual relationship with tabloid reporter Vincent Clarkson, portrayed by Phillip Jeanmarie. Chad initially did not realize that Vincent, intersex, was also Valerie Davis (played by Daphnee Duplaix), the executive assistant at Crane Industries. When confessing the affair to Paloma and Noah, Chad repeatedly insisted he was not gay, emphasizing the relationship as purely physical.

E!'s *The Soup* host Joel McHale famously turned Chad's repeated "I'm not gay!" protestations into a running gag, dubbing him "Not Gay Chad." Divins himself made a cameo on the show's season-five premiere, poking fun at the storyline.

Whitney, pregnant with their second child, grew increasingly suspicious. Vincent orchestrated a scheme in which Whitney discovered the two having sex in the back of a gay bar. Heartbroken, Whitney left Chad, and he began to distance himself from Vincent. Later, the estranged couple began reconciling while helping Theresa and Ethan reunite.

Their happily-ever-after, however, was tragically cut short on August 28, 2007. Chad heroically died protecting Ethan, professing his love for Whitney, Miles, and their unborn child.

The Chad-Vincent storyline made daytime history, marking the first depiction of two men having sex on a daytime soap. Though sensationalized by modern standards, it was one of the few depictions of male intimacy on daytime TV. Soapdom.com praised the plot for giving Charles Divins the chance to showcase his range, distinguishing him from his predecessor Donn Swaby. Critics and fans debated Chad's sexuality. The Advocate's Brent Hartinger called him a "closeted bisexual," while NewNowNext.com included Divins in its "Favorite Gay (Male) TV Character" poll.

Whitney mourned Chad's death and reflected on her own life. In a heartfelt conversation with Theresa, she decided it was time to start fresh outside of Harmony. The show highlighted their friendship through a touching montage spanning the entire series, mirroring the actresses' real-life bond.

Brook Kerr reflected, "We are still great friends to this day. It's been interesting because we've known each other for years and through so many phases of life, but there's always been this grounded, we see each other kind of bond that we've had. Even through the ebbs and flow of life, it always comes back around and I feel like she's always been there. What's interesting is we barely talk about work... we're talking about how each other's heart's doing, trying to help the other person feel better, like a true friendship. I'm really appreciative of that."

Lindsay added that their friendship was more like sisters—a sentiment echoing the tight bond shared by most of the cast, highlighting just how much being on set at *Passions* felt like family.

Throughout the series, Eve had grown suspicious that Chad might be her long-lost son with Julian, but the truth—that it was actually Vincent—rolled in a storm. Vincent soon revealed to both Eve and Julian that he was also the mysterious blackmailer, donning a half-man, half-woman disguise tormenting much of the town.

While viewers debated the storylines, the cast experienced the twists firsthand, discovering their characters' fates as the scripts arrived. Phillip Jeanmarie and Daphnee Duplaix later admitted they had no idea where their storylines were headed until they received scripts.

Critics and journalists weighed in on the daring plots. At the time, soap journalist Jamey Giddens praised Jeanmarie on *Daytime*

Confidential for making Vincent believable amid the sensational twists, writing, "If anyone on that show could have won an Emmy, it was him."

Josh Robertson at *Complex* highlighted Duplaix as one of the most successful Playboy Playmates to go on to have a successful career in soaps—not only on *Passions* but later as *One Life to Live's* Rachel Gannon. In 2025, Duplaix would shine in a leading role on CBS's *Beyond the Gates*, the first new daytime soap to debut on a major broadcast network since *Passions*.

When asked if NBC ever pushed back on Reilly's wild storylines, associate head writer Marlene McPherson said, "You know, there might have been, but Jim was in a position where he made it clear right at the start that he was not going to take notes from them. He said, 'No, I'm not going to be changing things. So you either take me as what I'm doing and let me do it, or I'm not doing the show.'"

Marlene recalled a meeting Jim and executive producer Lisa de Cazotte had with an NBC executive at the onset, "Jim said, 'Well, that's fine, because Lisa will *never* have any notes, will you, Lisa?' He was very pointed. He wasn't going to take other people's notes. After his experience on *Days*, he said, 'I'm not taking notes from people. I know what this show is. This is my vision, and I'm not going to let anybody fuck with it.'"

CHAPTER TWENTY-FIVE — *DirecTV Transition*

With the show navigating groundbreaking storylines and budget cuts, the next challenge was ensuring *Passions* survived beyond NBC's walls. As the NBC run neared its end, viewers wondered: could *Passions*, like Tabitha, who had literally been burned at the stake, cheat death?

Despite *The Today Show* expansion still looming, NBC executives remained impressed. The soap ranked fourth out of the nine remaining soaps among women aged 18–34, a prized demographic. NBC also fully owned *Passions,* keeping all profits from its production. It was a rare advantage in daytime television.

Because of its strong appeal among young women, rumors swirled that NBC was exploring ways to keep the show alive, possibly online or through Disney's SoapNet cable channel. Then came the shock announcement: *Passions* would survive through a $40 million deal with DirecTV.

In what became DirecTV's largest original programming venture to date, the satellite provider ordered a full season of new episodes from NBCUniversal, with production set to continue after the NBC run ended.

However, there were changes. *Passions* would now only air four days a week, Monday through Thursday. Its budget would shrink even more, by one-third, to around $700,000 per week. DirecTV would absorb all production costs—nearly $40 million over 52 weeks —and recoup a portion through advertising.

NBC executive Marc Graboff called the partnership a potential model for future collaborations, noting the network might package exclusive content for providers like DirecTV or Comcast. The strategy would soon repeat with NBC's *Friday Night Lights*.

Passions premiered that September on DirecTV's The 101 Network. The satellite provider now had a program with strong female appeal. Analysts noted that if just 25 percent of the show's loyal fanbase subscribed to DirecTV, the deal could easily pay for itself. In its final NBC months, the show even winked at the transition, with Harmony homes suddenly sporting DirecTV dishes, and ads from the cast urging fans to call and subscribe to the satellite provider.

Associate head writer Marlene McPherson admitted to us, "When we went to DirecTV, Jim didn't really want to go, but he didn't want everyone to lose their jobs, so he took the deal, which we all took enormous pay cuts. We went down basically to getting Writers Guild scale, I think even the actors were at scale. Jim said to me and Darrell Ray Thomas, 'I'm not going to continue to do this, I'll have you guys take over at some point. I need to stay here for a year and six months, and then you guys can take over.'"

In the end, it never came to pass. DirecTV's decision not to renew their deal with NBC for a second year brought the quiet succession plan to a close, which would have passed *Passions* into new hands. Jim's protégés, Marlene McPherson and Darrell Ray Thomas, were poised to take over as head writers, marking the first time anyone other than Jim would have shaped the lives—and scandals—of Harmony's citizens. Fans who had followed the show as Jim's singular vision would never see that new era. In the end, Jim remained at the helm, steering the series through its final chapter. It was the story he began, and ultimately, the one he would finish.

CHAPTER TWENTY-SIX — *Series Finale*

Passions aired its final episode on August 7, 2008. Though it became DirecTV's highest-rated original program, insiders say the satellite provider ultimately fell short of the new subscriber numbers it had hoped the soap's move from broadcast would deliver.

It was déjà vu for the cast and crew, only this time they were told that negotiations to save the show through another outlet had fallen through.

On screen, Theresa finally ended up with Ethan after the long-awaited revelation that it was Gwen and Rebecca who had leaked the tabloid story. It was a fairytale ending, one that rewarded years of longing, heartbreak, and hope. In the final moments, Theresa and Ethan turned to the camera as she delivered one last message over the shows theme song:

"So after all these years, I've learned one thing for sure: always follow your passion—because that, and that alone, will lead you to your happy ending."

As confetti and balloons fell, the cast waved to the audience, with Tabitha holding a framed picture of Timmy, a touching tribute to Josh Ryan Evans and the joy he brought to the show. What followed next was a message on screen:

"From all of us to all of you... Thank you."

Moments later, the crew joined the cast on set, clapping and cheering as Josh Ryan Evans' voice filled the air, singing "Auld Lang

Syne." It was more than a goodbye—it was a celebration of everything *Passions* had stood for: heart, imagination, and risk.

Tracey Ross shared how the moment didn't feel real, as if they were waiving goodbye but would come back the next day like 'We fooled ya!'

Lindsay Hartley shared how her experience on the show was like bootcamp, preparing her for her career now as a writer, having sold six movies to Lifetime and having just directed her first film.

Eric Martsolf added, "To this day, I feel guilty about getting paid to be on *Passions* because it was just such a great time. There was a little bit of work involved, obviously, but what a great group of people and what a great time in my life. And I knew after a couple months of doing that show that this is what I wanted to do for a living. And as I sit here right now, I'm still on NBC Daytime. So yeah, I got suckered into it and I still love it."

Eric now plays Brady on NBC's *Days of our Lives*.

He noted, "I still have folks coming up to me at *Days of Our Lives* events talking about *Passions* and how much they miss the pure escapism. And it allowed people to just let go of their lives for a minute and just dive into whatever the heck we were doing that day."

Even after the finale, Harmony lived on—fans continued to upload episodes, attend reunions, and share tributes.

During its original run, *Passions* fostered one of the most devoted fan communities in daytime television. Members of the official fan club received autographed cast photos, biannual newsletters, exclusive merchandise, and invitations to fan luncheons. The show even dropped the official recipes to the Martimmy drink and Grace's Tomato Soup Cake! The show's official charity was St. Margaret Mary's Catholic School in the Bronx, a name that Jim Reilly borrowed for the fictional St. Margaret Mary's Church in Harmony, where Father Lonigan presided over Christmas masses, weddings, and countless dramatic revelations, even the ones interrupted by Ivy's car.

At the height of its popularity, the cast appeared on special episodes of NBC's *The Weakest Link*, and battled against the cast of *Days of our Lives* on *Family Feud*, then-hosted by Louie Anderson, among other game show and talk show appearances.

Even through its DirecTV run, the magic of Harmony endured. The final credits may have rolled, but the story never really ended. For millions of fans, Harmony still feels like home.

When Galen Gering looks back at the original cast photo, he laughs.

"Oh my god, we were like babies, we were like kids. I was 29, but there were people who were literally 17, 18, 19, 20. Not that you're not still growing at 29, I still had so much to learn. A lot of people just grew up... those ten years were so important, not only in terms of age, but because so much was happening in our lives. We were on this show, and for the most part everyone really kept their shit together, all things considered. That was pretty great too. Looking back, I think a lot of people have really fond memories of that show and that time."

Even years after the show ended, *Passions* continued to shape lives, inspiring creativity far beyond its screens. Reflecting on how the show inspired her to become an author, *New York Times* bestselling author Angie Thomas shared her thoughts with palpable enthusiasm:

"A lot of times people ask me what made me become a writer," she said. "And I always surprise them. I don't tell them I read these books or that I studied literature — I tell them I started writing *Passions* fan fiction. And people are like, 'Oh my God, I loved that show!' I've had so many of those conversations over the years — people saying they wish it was still on, or remembering scenes and characters in detail. Even now, on Twitter, I talk with fans all the time. The fan base is still passionate about *Passions*."

"This is a show that does not get enough credit," Angie continues. "There's a lot happening in television right now that *Passions* started. They were trailblazers in so many ways. If *Passions* debuted today on a streamer, it would be huge. You think *Stranger Things* is big? A lot of that is *Passions*! That whole town is Harmony. We still see pieces of what *Passions* did — it's alive and well now. If rebooted, that show would absolutely have a fan base."

And behind it all was one man: the dreamer who dared to make daytime weird, wild, and wonderful. The story of Jim Reilly, his imagination, his faith, and his fire was as bold as Harmony itself.

CHAPTER TWENTY-SEVEN — *Legacy*

Just two months after *Passions* aired its final episode, the man who had poured his heart, soul, and boundless creativity into every unforgettable moment, James E. Reilly, was gone. He died on October 12, 2008, at a New York City hospital from complications following cardiac surgery. He was 60 years old. His longtime agent and friend of 25 years, Jonathan Russo, confirmed the news, adding that Reilly had been recovering from surgery when he passed suddenly, with his beloved sister, Cathy Robinson, at his side, a quiet witness to the life he poured into the world.

Russo reflected after his passing, "James Reilly was one of the most profoundly lovely human beings in our industry. He was a towering figure who had a tremendous faith in God and Catholicism, as anyone who watched *Passions* knows. Everyone will miss him."

Executive producer Lisa de Cazotte also shared, "Jim Reilly was not only a legend in our industry, but he was a great friend and mentor. His creativity, sense of humor, and genius will be sorely missed. There will never be another like him, and I am deeply grateful for the years we spent working together on *Passions* and for the joy he brought to my life."

A decade later, the family of *Passions* mourned again. Lisa de Cazotte passed away on December 7, 2019, after a long illness. Not long after, her right hand, Richard Schilling, died on August 18, 2020, at age 56, marking the end of an era for the team who had brought Harmony to life.

Marlene McPherson said, her voice filled with awe "It was the best, best, hands-down best show I've ever worked on in my life. Jim was the most rare, incredible person. He was the kindest person you could ever meet, ever. He was generous, he was kind, he loved telling stories. He could talk for hours, he could entertain you for hours. He truly loved his family, and there was just no one like him."

Darrell Ray Thomas echoed that sentiment, his eyes misting as he spoke of Jim. "He put so much of himself into the show. He really wanted the fans to enjoy it, he wasn't going to just pander and give them whatever they wanted. He was going to give them an exciting, interesting, crazy, out-there, enjoyable show that kept them coming back. When they got home from work or class, for that hour nothing else mattered. They got taken away to the demon closet, they got lost in Luis and Sheridan on the Titanic, they went to prom with Charity as the boat sank, and they forgot about their lives that might've been troubling or difficult, they were entertained for an hour." He choked up with emotion. "And I just wish they knew how much the show meant to him, how much he put into it, and how much he loved the fans."

Though they are gone, the creativity, heart, and devotion of Jim, Lisa, and Richard continue to live on in the hearts of fans, a testament to the joy and wonder they brought to the world.

A TRIBUTE — *Slipping Away*

When Galen Gering sat down for his interview, before we even began, he leaned forward and asked, "I have a question for you, what about Ben Masters?" referring to the actor who played Julian Crane. He looked disappointed when we told him no one knew where Ben was. "Son of a bitch. He's like a missing person," he joked, shaking his head. "Anyway, he meant a lot to me, really helped me a lot, and is a great dude, so..."

He went on to recall their first meeting. "When I first went in to screen test, I tested with McKenzie and Ben. McKenzie was so cool and we obviously had chemistry and the whole thing, but Ben was so freaking good that all of a sudden I was watching him in the scene and was like, wait, what's happening? He's just doing all this interesting stuff, not how I foresaw this scene going at all. I started going off my lines, then literally, cut to like five takes later, and I was like, ah, shit, well, I blew that. I ended up getting it, and he was someone who helped me out a lot as an actor. We used to have these great talks, and obviously he had so much knowledge and wealth to give in that department. Forever grateful, so I'd love to see him."

Ben Masters and Kim Johnston Ulrich had worked together years earlier on *Murder, She Wrote* in a 1994 episode titled "The Trouble with Seth," delivering stellar performances before becoming husband and wife on *Passions*. Kim Johnston Ulrich, who played Ivy Crane, recalled, "Ben was wonderful to work with. He was very professional, a very good actor, had done a lot of work, and was the biggest curmudgeon in the world," she said, laughing, "but fun and respectful to work with."

Amelia Marshall, who played Liz Sanborne, added, "Ben always had something up his sleeve. No matter what was on the page, what the through line of that particular scene was, there was always a wrinkle that he would introduce. As an actor, that just made it fun. It's like, okay, what's he going to do? I'd kind of glare at him and go, 'Oh, that's your take today.' And he would save it for tape, and every scene I had with him was just delightful."

His mysterious disappearance was commented on several times by various cast members, with some even saying, "It's like he fell off the earth."

Remembering the fun times, Andrea Evans recalled a scene where she was standing at a coffee table and Ben was sitting on a couch. "I was supposed to go pick something up, so I kind of made a conscious decision, even though I was blocking him a little bit. I just bent down, and my butt was right in his face. The look on his face was just hysterical. It was spontaneous, and I was just doing what I thought the character would do."

Eric Martsolf remembered another moment on set. "I was having trouble with my monologue, and I was like, 'I can't believe I'm talking to myself and saying this.' And he's like, 'Son, don't read the lines, read your check.'" Eric laughed as he recalled Ben's humor and favorite sayings. "He was very practical, and a very good man."

Eric told us he hopes Ben is happy wherever he is and that he misses him. Lindsay Hartley agreed, adding, "We love you."

No one was more candid or emotional about Ben than Tracey Ross, who played Eve Russell. She was also disappointed to hear that no one had been in contact with him. "He's just disappeared as far as I know," she said. "I've phoned him, I've written him, I sent him back his leather jacket that he was looking for. And my son and my son's two friends loved him. They kind of, for four years, grew up there with Ben, and they asked all the time, 'Where's Ben? When are we going to see Ben?' And I was like, 'Ben is just not communicating. I don't know why. Those boys loved him.'"

She continued, "All three of them, Chris, Dan, and my son, Bryce, are all doing extremely well now, and they want to show Ben how well they're doing. They want Ben to be part of it. They want to say, 'Hey, Ben, look at this. Ben, come here,' they loved Ben. And two of them have their own show coming on Animal Planet, 22 episodes, called *Barn Sanctuary*. The two brothers who lived with me their last two years of school because their parents went back to Michigan, and were best friends with my son. So all three of those boys lived in the same house and saw Ben all the time. And my son Bryce (known professionally as Bryce Vine) is doing really well with a solo performing artist career."

"They want to show off and say, 'Ben, aren't you proud of us? They want Ben to slap them on the shoulder and say, 'Boy, you guys did good,' and he won't. And I don't know if he doesn't understand, and you don't know what's going on in people's lives, but we all love Ben. Everybody loves Ben. And he deserves it. And he was the most fun I ever had in a relationship, and the most I ever laughed.'"

"I call them my sons...but I think my son, and Chris and Dan... I think we're just going to all go one day and just cover all the entrances and exits around his house and say, 'We know you're in there, we're not leaving till you come out,'" she added with a laugh.

None of them could have known what would come next. Tragically, not long after these interviews, the mystery surrounding Ben Masters reached its heartbreaking conclusion. On January 11, 2023, it was announced that Ben Masters had passed away at the age of 75, from complications of COVID-19 after a private struggle with dementia. The mystery that had surrounded his disappearance now felt achingly clear. He had been slipping away long before anyone realized.

Andrea Evans would pass away nearly six months later due to breast cancer at 66. Before her passing, she shared with us she was meant to do *Passions*. She elaborated, using her scene with the boa constrictor wrapped around her as an example, "You had all these big, burly men that were working behind the scenes, and they had to leave the room. The reason I wasn't bothered by it is because I used to ride elephants for the circus, truthfully, for *Ringling Brothers, Barnum & Bailey*, and my grandmother worked in carnivals and worked in the circus. So, I had no fear of such trained animals because I kind of grew up with that. So, the boa constrictor did not bother me at all. In fact, I have a picture of my daughter with a boa constrictor wrapped around her. A little secret. I was meant to do that show," she laughed, a wink at how outrageous the show could be.

Bruce French, who played Father Lonigan, would lose his battle with Alzheimer's at 79. His wife of 34 years was longtime *Days of Our Lives* actress Eileen Barnett.

At the time of our interviews, Ben Masters' whereabouts were unknown, and much of the cast's memories naturally centered on him. Andrea Evans and Bruce French, whose contributions were equally treasured, would pass away months later, leaving a lasting impact on all who knew them.

For the cast, crew, and fans who loved them and the memories they created, Harmony lives on. They are now angels in the upper room, having a meet-up with Jim and Lisa, surrounded by their beloved *Passions* family, sharing a quiet, timeless moment together. Harmony endures, a bridge to the world that awaits in the epilogue.

EPILOGUE — *Last Call at the Crane Mansion*

You didn't think we'd end without one last Martimmy, did you?

Harmony has always had a funny way of looping back on itself — spells broken, hearts resurrected, villains reformed only to relapse by the next commercial break. You could say the town was cursed. I prefer to think of it as *eternal*.

The truth is, *Passions* never really died. Sure, DirecTV didn't pick up another year, the sets were struck, and the studio lights dimmed. But somewhere — in a thousand YouTube uploads (hey NBC, it's time to release the show on your streamer Peacock, just saying), in the memories of fans who still hum Jane French's lullaby— Harmony keeps breathing.
Breathe in. Breathe out.

Maybe that's why I'm back, one last time. J.T. Cornell, your favorite gossip ghoul, fresh out of the grave and still armed with a Martimmy and a headline. I've shown you the spells and the scandals, the love and the lunacy. I've introduced you to the dreamers who risked their careers on a show that made daytime feel dangerous again.

James E. Reilly made us care about witches, dolls, demons, mermaids, and endless weddings interrupted — but he also gave us permission to feel everything at once. Laugh. Cry. Gasp. Roll your eyes. Come back tomorrow.

And that's what *Passions* really was — an invitation to feel.

Lisa de Cazotte made sure it looked like magic. The cast gave it heart. And you — the fans — kept it alive long after the last credits rolled. As the theme song said, *you are the fire burning*. Every tweet, every rewatch, every "remember when Tabitha and Timmy—?" moment was another pulse of life in a show that refused to stay buried.

So here's to the witches, the angels, the sinners, and the fools. To the actors who believed, the writers who dared, and the viewers who never stopped watching...

Here's to the scandal-plagued Cranes, the lovesick Lopez-Fitzgeralds, the ambitious Russells, and Tabitha's pain-in-the-neck next-door neighbors, the Bennetts...

And here's to you — for daring to open this book and go back to Harmony.

The lava's cooled, the volcano's quiet, and the town sleeps again. But if you listen closely, you can still hear the theme song echoing through the mist of the New England harbor.

You are my passion for life.

We're always coming back to Harmony.

— *J.T. Cornell*

www.ingramcontent.com/pod-product-compliance
Lightning Source LLC
Chambersburg PA
CBHW020741130626
46554CB00006B/2083